... and That's the Way

My Cookies Crumble

By Ellen Waterfield

Cheers,
Ellen

ISBN Print 978-1-989848-25-8

ISBN Ebook 978-1-989848-26-5

Dedication

I dedicate this, my first book, to my precious mom, Edith, who was the most thoughtful, caring, and selfless human being I have ever known.
She loved me and shaped me to strive to seek happiness.
Her kind heart, beaming smile, and engaging laughter brought joy to many.
She passed away much too soon and is forever remembered.

Foreword

Ellen is a remarkable person. If anyone has the right to write, … *and That's the Way My Cookies Crumble*, which is all about kindness, gratitude, courage, and service, it is Ellen. These short, true cookie-based anecdotes tell a very human story of overcoming difficulties and realizing unexpected achievements. This gentle, generous, and delightfully caring woman lives life courageously and joyously. I am honoured to have been asked to write the foreword for her book.

When Ellen first mentioned that she had a manuscript about cookies, I hoped it would speak to the range and depth of her being. Her cookies indeed played a role in taking her on an unexpected journey of self-discovery and personal triumph. They became a connective and touching mechanism demonstrating that kindness and gratitude cultivate a sense of well-being. I witnessed her begin to reach out for that which was, to all appearances, beyond her grasp, only to discover that a purposeful, fulfilling life was well within her means. I am reminded of Pete Seeger's song, "We Shall Overcome" Her cookie stories provide a framework for describing her personal trajectory.

Through the years, I saw Ellen forge ahead, leaving behind those smaller, harsher times she describes in her book. Committed to overcoming her fears, she set personal goals and steadfastly faced any and all unimaginable future challenges.

CHILDHOOD

The height of a mountain is measured at its root, and one could say the same about our childhoods. In her own words, Ellen tells us, "A little girl, who could have lived, struggled, and died in her own limited little world, got to see and feel the world in a bigger way."

KARATE

I met Ellen decades ago when she started karate. Her young son Marc had started training first for confidence building. Then, several years later she began. Her generous spirit soon made its presence felt in the dojo. She gave her energy and time to the study of karate as well as our seasonal celebrations and fundraisers. Ellen and I became friends, as she describes in the Karate Influence and Growth chapter.

She was always there to lend a hand. In writing this foreword, I asked a friend and former classmate what she thought of Ellen's contribution. She said, "Ellen was the quintessential team builder and the glue that held the dojo together, dedicated to every task she undertook." The arc of her life shows a strength, as well as a resolve to find a better way forward for herself and those around her. Her kindness and gratitude represented by her cookies is a signature quality of Ellen. One we all need more of in our daily lives.

Ellen's achievements go well beyond her training and belt levels, her qualifications, or whatever her intentions were when she first walked into the dojo.

TRAVEL

When Ellen found herself on her own with her two teenage children, she continued to support them in their interests and the goals they set. Eventually she began offering her home to foreign students, building relationships and creating lifelong friendships. This turned her into a world traveller. As she says, "My friends made it possible for me to grow and travel throughout the world not as a tourist but as a fellow traveller."

In her words, "Kindness and gratitude opened many doors for me to walk through …"

Ellen's cookie stories take the reader on a delightful life adventure of transformation and global travel. Her book, … *and That's the Way My Cookies Crumble* is the sweetest of treats, a story of kindness, generosity, and service to others.

Augusta

Fall 2020

Author of **Moments That Blink Back** and **The Cottage Woman** being published in 2021.

Message from the Author

I struggled throughout my life with insecurity and low self-esteem and became exceptionally good at masking this with humour and lots of talking. Early on, I had committed my life to being a pleaser, focusing on the needs of others, never my own. Then I found myself at an all-time low struggling with the death of my dear mom.

Without the influence of significant people who came into my life, I would not be the person I have become. Each one inspired me to go far beyond what I perceived to be my limitations.

At sixty-nine and on my own, I purchased a one-way ticket to Calgary, Alberta. I had often flown east to west from Nova Scotia to spend precious time with my daughter, her husband, and my three adorable grandchildren. This visit would include time spent re-evaluating my life and making important decisions.

My daughter welcomed me and supported my time-out frame of mind. Unbelievably, a month before my arrival, she spotted a room-for-rent ad in her growing community of Legacy. We agreed that she check it out. Almighty Fate had presented me with a living space just a 3-minute walk from my daughter's home. We could enjoy being there for each other in every way without sacrificing our privacy. Not homeless, but without a home of my own, I began to write this book.

In Part I, I focus on 'the makings of my cookies'. Over the years, my peanut butter chocolate chip cookies have been enjoyed by family and friends. I began gifting them on special occasions, and then gave them to people as a token of my gratitude.

This began to snowball into countless true stories to be told. Some are sprinkled with heartache while others are dusted with surprises and enriching encounters.

In Part II, I focus on 'the making of me'. It is filled with precious memories, unexpected events in my life and the rewards of digging deep.

My love of baking made me aware that a leavening agent is of great importance to make my goods rise. I discovered that it was a perfect metaphor of how connecting with positive people had helped me to rise above my difficulties and despair. I now think of those people as my personal leavening agents. Their influence and support continues to inspire me to seek out and savour the sweet taste that life has to offer.

My stories and experiences as told in this book are not in chronological order.

My message is that simple acts of gratitude and kindness can lift our spirits high.

Table of Contents

PART I

… the makings of my cookies

PART II

… the making of me

PART I

... the makings of my cookies

Chapter 1:
The Gifts That Keep On Giving

For sure, heartfelt gift-giving can be a joyful experience for both the giver and the recipient. However, it isn't always easy to decide *what* to give, especially when your cash flow is minimal. If I wanted to offer great gifts that everyone enjoyed, I had to be resourceful.

It was my parents' wedding anniversary. For this celebration my mom had baked her popular, mouth-watering homemade bread, and I had made my peanut butter chocolate chip cookies. My gift was in a long floral box tied with a bright red ribbon. After reading the card, my mom opened the box. She glowed seeing its contents, then did a double take. With a wily smile, she said to my dad, "Stan, you're really going to like these flowers."

My dad was distracted getting another gift for her to open, but, seeing her riveted, he decided to take a quick glance. Then, he too was smiling. They looked at each other like two kids in a candy store. My dad tended to not be camera-friendly, so it shocked me to hear him say, "Edith, give me the box. Ellen, get a photo of this." He took the box from her, cradling it close and tilting it slightly up so we could see his free hand inside, touching its contents. I took a treasured photo.

Upon closer inspection, it was clear these were not fresh flowers. Instead, I had made twelve long-stemmed roses out of money and nestled them among greenery and baby's breath. The petals were various denominations of colourful one, two, and five-dollar bills. It was an insignificant amount of money, but rich with sentiment and the surprise factor. My mom happily put them in a vase.

The joy of that experience proved I didn't need a lot of money to give someone a nice gift. I went on to continue to tap into my creativity, coming up with more handcrafted gifts which included personalized occasion cards with a blast from the past photo or two. What had started as a resourceful workaround, turned into a fun activity. Another fond gift-giving memory involved two precious little girls.

My niece and her husband decided it was time to get a bigger house to accommodate the needs of their growing family. They found a perfect three-level home with a good-sized backyard. Also, there was an elementary school within walking distance for their girls. The whole family was delighted to begin a new chapter together.

Brown-haired, blue-eyed Katie loved being Abbi's big sister. Together they found fun and magic in each day. I decided to give them their own special housewarming gift.

Out I went to shop for what I needed to bring a smile to their little faces. I found two inexpensive doggie bowls that would be perfect for what I had in mind. One was white with several cute Dalmatian puppies on it, and the other featured the cartoon world's popular dog of-the-day. Rather than dog treats, they would be filled high to the sky with the girls' favourite cookies, made by me with love.

I used cellophane for the cookie doggie bowls to be visible, just like fruit baskets. One was tied with bright pink and blue ribbons cascading down while the other was

4

colour coordinated with the black and white of the Dalmatians. I was pleased with the overall results; these gifts were unique and yummy. Also, the bowls just might come in handy in the future if the family decided to add a puppy to the mix.

The day finally came when these sweet girls saw the beautifully wrapped surprises, I had for them. They literally jumped for joy and showered me with heartfelt hugs. I saw that their mom and dad were enchanted by their daughters' obvious delight.

Katie sat at the kitchen table and immediately began eating the cookies while her little sister put her bowl on the floor and started acting like a frisky little puppy, biting and licking the chocolate chips. Abbi's auburn curly hair and eye color were, in fact, very puppy-like. It was a hoot to see.

After a day or two, Abbi's mom, joining in the game, put her little girl's bowl on the table and said, "Sit girl. Eat!" and she did just that. Those doggie bowls would go on to be used for cereal, fruit, and snacks of Goldfish crackers.

A few months later, Katie and Abbi were in my kitchen, excitedly making a batch of my cookies for the first time. They placed them on a special dessert dish for our fancy tea party.

As they grew, the girls began measuring to see how close they were to becoming taller than me. Both happily achieved their goal around age eleven. I have a hilarious memory of sitting on a stool in their living room and looking out the window. I felt arms being slipped under mine from behind, and as I turned, my feet were gathered up in one fell swoop. The timing and execution were fast and flawless, as Katie and Abbi transported me across the room.

Their mom laughed so hard she needed a minute before saying, "Put her down." They deposited me safely on the sofa. Katie had taken my upper body while Abbi supported my legs. They were ecstatic to have pulled it off. As for me, I knew then what it was like to be swept off my feet!

When I moved to another province, I missed the antics of these girls. Then one day, I received the exciting news that they had got a puppy. Katie, being a teenager, told me she was not really on board so much while younger Abbi was thrilled. It was Abbi who named the cuddly eight-week old Golden Retriever, Piper, and promised to take care of her every need. Despite the best of intentions, her commitment wavered. Always there for each other, her mom and Katie gave a helping hand. Piper is a treasured member of the family. She receives and gives much love. If Abbi is feeling unwell or stressed, Piper brings a whole lot of comfort her way.

It is my experience that, whether given or received, heartfelt gifts and happy times spent together create wonderful memories to cherish for a lifetime.

Chapter 2:
My Lost Christmas of Long Ago

Over the years, I had begun the habit of bringing my cookies to my favourite bank teller. I appreciated the convenience of on-line banking, but still enjoyed making the occasional in person visit. On one of my frequent daily walks, I planned to drop by the bank, deposit a cheque, and pick up a calendar to bring in the fast-approaching new year. This gave me the opportunity to deliver some cookies stowed in my trusty denim backpack.

Year-round, I enjoyed the sights and aromas of my favourite woodsy trail. I was entertained by the sound of the birds singing, bees buzzing, and the little forest critters scurrying about. All were engaged in their own busyness.

Mother Nature offered me her finest in-season specials of scented rose bushes, clusters of mayflowers, stately lady slippers, and other beautifully colored flowers. An abundance of leafy trees, firs, and pines claimed their space. At harvest time, I enjoyed wild blueberries, blackberries, raspberries and strawberries for baking or to sprinkle on my cereal. Autumn's brilliant colors and Winter's coat of snow were always a wondrous sight to behold.

I arrived at the bank, took my place in line, and spotted Irene. Her curly blonde hair framed her vivid blue eyes. She was with a client, so I invited people to go ahead of me and waited for her. If time permitted, Irene and I shared the goings-on of our families.

On this day, she turned to her colleagues and said, "Here comes my Cookie Lady." I loved her smile and spontaneous sense of humour. They responded jokingly with, "You have to share." The bag, tied with curly ribbons, held four cookies, so she cheerfully agreed. I decided it was best to bring more next time. With my fingers crossed, I asked Irene for a calendar. Again, my tardiness was tested.

Three tellers began to search. Two returned empty handed, but the third arrived triumphantly holding one. She announced, "This is the last one and it's yours." I was leaving, grateful to all and adamant to never be in this situation again.

Making my way outside, I met an elderly woman. Her gray hair was neatly pulled up in a bun and she appeared to be on a mission. She thanked me for holding the door open, then paused, eyeing the treasure held firmly in my hand. I felt like a deer in the headlights when she said that she was there to get her calendar. When I confessed that I had the last one, she sighed, and her demeanor changed. She said, "My husband is waiting in the car, and he won't be happy about this." The tone of her voice was disturbing. I sensed she might get a lecture that would ruin her day. Without a moment's hesitation, I told her she could have mine.

She thanked me and said it was meant for me, not her. I held it out saying it was a gift from me. Her sad brown eyes brightened with relief as she carefully placed it in her shopping bag. I wished I had some cookies to give her as well, but alas, my backpack was empty. As I watched this woman hasten to the waiting car, a lost memory of mine began to surface.

*****

When I was a child, every Christmas came with the promise of being rewarded for the efforts put into being good little boys and girls. God, our parents, and Santa wanted us to do what we were told, be kind and not tell lies. Each year, as December 25th neared, I became giddy with anticipation. I knew my friends got much more than I did, but the truth was that Santa never let me down.

My dad would not allow a spruce tree to darken our door. According to him, their needles fall quickly to the floor. Our Christmas tree was, without fail, a mighty fir and usually tucked in the same corner. Dad fastened it on both sides with a thick cord, and it would be kept fresh standing in a water-filled container. If he thought it needed a touch-up, he would call out: "Get me my saw." The tree would shake as if in a windstorm while he removed and relocated branches to his liking. Then my dad would leave the room happy that *his* job was done.

My older brother, Gordie, took over getting our Christmas tree in his early teens. For five years, he went off, axe in hand, into the woods nearby. He would return with what we all thought was the perfect Christmas tree. The woodsy smell of the outdoor forest then filled our living room.

My mom would bring out boxes of Christmas decorations; a star for the top, ornaments, the golden garland, and the shiny silver tinsel. Importantly, first our Christmas tree lights would be wrapped around the tree from top to bottom. This would involve multiple strings attached to each other until there was enough. Once plugged in, the brilliant colours of red, green, blue, and yellow came alive.

My love of Christmas carols prompted me one year to try out for the church choir. Singers whose voices earned the teacher's praise were shown a special place to sit. When it was my turn, she listened, paused, and asked a few girls to sing along with me. She then bent down, patted my head, and said, "Maybe next year." I was disappointed at first, then I thought, *God gave me my voice so it couldn't be that bad.* Another memory was with friends gathered around, I sat on a stump in the forested area near our elementary school and blissfully sang a song. When I was finished, someone blurted out, "You're not a good singer, but you sure know all the words." This became a family joke, especially when we gathered around a campfire. Without fail, I would hear, 'Will someone find Ellen a stump'.

With no fireplace, we could not hang our Christmas stockings with care as the poem goes. Instead, they were placed at the foot of each bed. In the dark, feeling my stocking had been filled meant Santa had arrived. Santa did not bury us in toys; he left a few choice items that he knew would bring joy to each of us. Guns and holsters, dinky toys, and a new sled easily made my brothers happy, as did a much-wanted doll, dishes, and such for us girls.

Now I will share with you the Christmas memory that found its way back into my life.

This Christmas morning was filled with excitement and chaos. The knock on our kitchen door was unnoticed by everyone but our mom. She called out for me to come to the kitchen. I was surprised to find a little boy, maybe the age of five, standing in the doorway with messy hair and tattered clothing. It was common in those days to see children wearing rubber boots in winter if their parents had minimal income; he was one of them. I wanted to get back to the living room, but my mother told me to wait with the boy.

She hurried down the cellar steps, came back with some empty bottles in a bag, and gave them to the boy. I knew he could get money for them. While turning to leave, my mom asked, "What did Santa bring you for Christmas?" He looked up and said, "I got nothing from Santa."

My mom told me to get the two books that Santa had brought. When I returned, she said, "Ellen, give him one of those books." I could not believe my ears. They were *my* books!

I recall her saying that Santa must have gotten mixed up on his busy night and left two books under our Christmas tree by mistake. She said, "Ellen, *one* was meant for you." and to the boy she said, "The *other* was meant for you." His eyes widened, and he gave her a toothless grin. I think that was when I finally handed over one of my books.

At that time, I wouldn't understand the profound impact of my mom's actions. She was making sure that this little boy knew he was special, and that Santa had not forgotten him. He left much happier than when he had arrived, with a book in one hand and his bag of bottles in the other.

*****

A car horn in the distance brought me back from my reverie. As I walked home on that beautiful day, I was empty-handed, but my heart was overflowing with gratitude for the retrieval of such a precious memory.

The best gift I had received that Christmas was the lesson I got from my mom to be sensitive and kind to others in any way I could.

Chapter 3:
Automotive Garage Delight

In my teens, a guy named Donald offered to teach me how to drive his standard car. It did not go well. Under my control, it jerked spasmodically, and the gears cried out in pain. With patience worn, Donald winced at the grinding sound that was coming from the transmission and told me my lesson was over. He made it clear that because of me, his car had lost little teeth and that was not good. On that day my confidence was eroded, and I would only drive automatic cars.

It amazes me how car-savvy some people are. I cannot even identify most of the makes and models on the road, let alone figure out what's going on under the hood. The thought of driving a standard continues to give me chills, but I have to confess that as a passenger in a sporty standard, green Miata convertible, I tuned into another mindset. While enjoying a scenic autumn drive with a friend, his car, at times, raced up and down the MacKenzie Mountain (Cabot Trail) on its winding paved road. This was a thrill of a lifetime for me as each sharp turn was taken flawlessly. I felt gears constantly shifting and saw euphoria on the face of my friend. It was as if he and his car were one.

I am diligent when it comes to my vehicle's maintenance. Prior to the nasty winter weather approaching, I knew my car needed undercoating. To avoid paying high dealership costs, I decided to try an automotive garage near my residence. It operated on a 'no appointment necessary' drive-through concept.

The garage impressed me with its cleanliness and a welcoming greeting. I explained what needed to be done. Following that, I was told to return to my vehicle. It was indeed a pleasant surprise to be offered the newspaper of the day and a beverage while waiting for a bay to become available. As I drank my coffee and worked on my crossword puzzle, I thought, *So far so good!*

The staff was ready for me sooner than I expected. As I maneuvered my vehicle into place, a well-groomed, young fellow wearing gray coveralls, held his hand up signaling me to stop. He politely informed me that there was a highly qualified mechanic underneath who would do a great job for me. While the undercoating was being applied, he checked my car's oil and other fluids. He proudly announced that the complimentary top-ups were taken care of. This was most impressive.

When the bay door in front of me began to slide up, I knew my car was good to go. I continued to be impressed as I was told that my payment could conveniently be made while seated in my car. I made my payment, and then got the answers to two important questions. The young man was not allergic to peanuts, and he liked chocolate.

I promised to return with some of my homemade peanut butter chocolate chip cookies to show my appreciation. This young fellow was very surprised. In an attempt to maintain his professionalism, he politely said, "You really don't have to do that." I told him it was my pleasure and that I would be back the next day.

I arrived bright and early in the morning with a can of cookies and was quickly spotted by the young man. Wasting no time, I took the lid off and asked if he wanted to do a taste test. As he took his first bite, a head popped up like a prairie dog from the area where my car had been serviced. "I'm the one who worked under your car." he bellowed. Within moments, everyone in the garage began to gather to see what all the fuss was about. The feeling of our mutually shared gratitude was priceless.

Several months later, when my car's oil change was due, I returned to the same garage. This time I brought a larger batch of cookies ready for morning and afternoon coffee breaks. Once again, I received excellent service and it was obvious that my cookies were becoming a welcomed treat.

Early that evening, while seated at my computer, I saw a one-day promotion of a ten-dollar coffee gift card to be awarded when getting an oil change. I called to say that I had been in that morning and had not received the gift card. The gentleman on the phone explained the offer was formally redeemable at the time of service but to come back before closing, and hopefully there would be a gift card for me.

When I arrived, I was asked to wait to speak to the manager. He appeared to be in his forties, well-groomed, and casually dressed in a denim shirt and jeans. He said, unfortunately, the gift cards were all gone. As soon as the words left his lips, one of the garage attendants approached and whispered in his ear.

The manager turned to me and said, "So, you're the Cookie Lady." He asked me to wait a moment and went back into his office. When he returned, I saw a small card in his hand. He told me my next oil change would be free and placed that card in my hand. I was stunned. The oil change for my car was specific and expensive.

There was a possibility that I would move before my next oil change, but, rather than saying so, I chose to enjoy the moment. I looked this generous man in the eyes and wholeheartedly thanked him. As I was about to leave, he said, "Just want to let you know your cookies are really good and they've been the talk of the garage. Thanks for doing that." Hearing this from him was a great way to end my day.

Circumstances put my move on hold, and fortunately, the card I had kept as a keepsake would find its way back to that garage. Once again, I brought some cookies to show my appreciation. I placed one container at the coffee station and then asked to see the manager to deliver his personally. I was disappointed to hear he had gone for lunch, but his cookies would be waiting for him on his desk.

With my oil change done, I was given the paperwork along with the unexpected news that there was a nail in one of my tires. When I asked to have it taken care of, I was unnerved to hear they might not carry the required patch. That's when the manager returned and recognized me. I immediately thanked him again for my free oil change and explained my unforeseen dilemma.

He got the mechanic to double-check and said that if they did not have the patch, he would go out to get one. I was warmed by this man's unlimited kindness and was totally relieved my tire would be fixed before I left.

The manager's response to my inquiry regarding the cost was unforgettable. He chuckled and said, "Your money is no good here, but your cookies are." Laughter rang out from everyone within earshot. He enjoyed his audience's reaction, as did I.

A few months later, I returned to this outstanding garage. It was not for another service but to deliver my last batch of homemade cookies and the message that I was on the move. I felt it was important to thank everyone for their stellar workmanship and the best customer service ever!

I will always remember that amazing team. Their example demonstrates that no matter what we choose to do in life, if we show up as our best selves and give it our all, the rewards are limitless.

Chapter 4:
A Ray of Sunshine
On a Routine Flight

Flying became a way of life for me once my son moved to Kumamoto and my daughter moved to Calgary. An encounter with a passenger on one of my flights to Calgary would bring me joy.

With my seatbelt snugly fastened, I sat back watching the last passengers board the plane. A tall, slim, young man with black-rimmed glasses was making his way down the narrow aisle. He wore a grey hoodie, black jeans, and a skateboard hat perched askew on his head. Super-sized headphones were around his neck. Then I saw the computer bag hanging from his shoulder that he steadied with one hand while his other hand maintained a tight grip on his cellphone.

When he finally reached his aisle seat, it was in my row. The middle seat remained vacant which made it easier for him to organize his belongings while I looked out my window. When I heard the click of his seat belt, I turned his way and we exchanged smiles. He had removed his hat and headphones. We remained silent until the plane taxied to the runway and stopped. It was then the young man politely introduced himself and asked if he could look out the window during take-off. We shared that we both enjoyed the thrill of a plane leaving the ground and climbing upward.

I always looked forward to getting a brief glimpse of some of my province of Nova Scotia from the air. The outlying farmlands and scattering of lakes and forested areas were plentiful. In this moment, we both gaped at the wonder of it all and agreed that this too was an adrenalin rush.

He removed his glasses, reclined in his seat, and drifted off to sleep. Later on, when the friendly flight attendant came by offering beverages, his eyes opened as if on cue. He ordered a soft drink and found his big bag of brilliant orange Cheetos that was in his backpack. When I offered my cookies, he quickly responded saying that they contained two of his favourite ingredients. I knew my grandchildren would not mind sharing the cookies I had baked for them.

Ray told me he was on his way to Calgary to pursue his studies in journalism. He said that information being given to the public was becoming laced with too much drama, speculation, and finger-pointing and that some of it could needlessly promote instant stress, panic, and rage. He wanted to give people the opportunity to process accurate information objectively. I complimented him on his great attitude.

With cookie in hand, he changed the subject and told me he wasn't married but looked forward to someday having a family. Ray wanted his children to be happy and to enjoy their lives.

This certainly was an enlightening interaction. He confided he was generally a private and cautious guy and that he was enjoying the ease he felt with me. I have had many enjoyable conversations over the course of my travels and this one was outstanding.

Obviously, our ages were far apart but we completely agreed that it was important to be aware, to communicate, and to use technology wisely.

He shook his head ruefully and confessed, "I did something totally out of character." He paused as if contemplating whether to continue or not. Then he told me that one day, while driving with his girlfriend at his side, he wanted to discuss something important but had to wait until she was off her cellphone. When no longer distracted by her device, he proceeded to say what was on his mind. During this, she became re-engaged with her cellphone. Sheepishly he said, "I couldn't believe she did that. It hurt me, so I took the phone from her hand and threw it out my window."

He must have seen my eyes grow wide, so he quickly explained that it was a reflex action that he instantly regretted. Ray then added, he had her complete attention, so he pulled his car over and turned off its engine. His girlfriend listened intently and said she understood where he was coming from. It was great to hear their talk ended on a positive note.

When the pilot announced we had begun our descent, I excused myself and headed to the washroom to get ready to meet my daughter and grandchildren who were waiting in the airport. I was excited to see them, but also felt a twinge of sadness that I, no doubt, would never see Ray again.

We shared the window view for one last time, taking in the spectacular sight of Calgary's high-rise tower, popular

Saddle Dome, and other iconic buildings. Our touchdown was smooth.

As the plane taxied to the gate, I told Ray how grateful I was that our paths had crossed, and he echoed the same sentiment. Then I offered him another cookie for the road, which he gladly stowed in his backpack. When the plane finally came to a halt, Ray stood up and then offered to get my carry-on from the overhead compartment. He indeed was a sensitive, caring young man.

I could not resist asking him what happened to the cellphone he had tossed. He chuckled and said that he was driving slowly at the time and saw it fly into a hedge. It was good to know that the phone had not been damaged and their relationship flourished.

Chapter 5:
Heartfelt Flea Market Moments

I came to know Bob in my mid-sixties. Being a veteran flea market fan, he invited me to join him on a number of occasions. I got to meet his son, Kevin, his daughter-in-law, Michelle and their three teenage sons. Instantly each one captured my heart. Their children, like my son and daughter, set goals early on in life, got part-time jobs and worked hard to make their dreams come true.

I was told Ethan, their first-born, arrived in the world with a smile on his face and a heart of gold. From his early childhood, he banged on any surface he could find. Eventually Ethan got a drum set. Like his Grampie Bob, he was enthralled with cars. Overtime with his savings, he proudly bought his first car. This young man gathers information on a variety of makes and models and gladly shares it with family and friends. He is a valued employee in a store with an automotive department and aspires to become a skilful mechanic.

Michelle said that when Alex came along, "He was born high-spirited and humble." Bob's dad, fondly known as Pop, dedicated his life to proudly serve in the Navy. Alex idealized his great-grandfather and, at seventeen, became a Naval Reservist. It was nice to witness his induction ceremony. Alex's reservist experiences include valuable sea time aboard HMCS Harry DeWolfe. I am sure when he decides to commit to a career, it will be one that makes him happy. Like his older brother, he decided to play a musical instrument; he chose a bass guitar.

Ambitious Evan came along to complete the trio. When he was seven, he received a guitar for Christmas. His mom told me, "The right-handed instrument wasn't really appropriate for our leftie child, but for him it wasn't an issue." Evan set his mind on honing his electric guitar skills. At fifteen, his hard work paid off. A talent scout saw him perform, generating multiple scholarships from the renowned Berklee College of Music. Evan is focused on a career in music. I am sure his musical talent will bring delight to many.

Kevin, the proud dad of his amazing sons, had learned to play a few chords on the guitar at an early age. It soon became apparent that he could play by ear. Along with an established career, he continued to make time for his passion of playing the electric guitar. His influence impacted his sons and together they formed a family band providing welcomed entertainment at community functions. This would lead to many musical opportunities, one being Kevin becoming a member of the 'Saving Sweet Polly' band. I was thrilled to attend an awesome performance.

Michelle selflessly gives to her family. This includes her love, time, energy, and skillful support for her guys' musical endeavours. With heartfelt love and appreciation, they gave her the title of Momager. She told me she wants to, "lift her sons higher in life, to help them see their uniqueness and special place in this world. When together, we enjoyed friendship, music, and cookies.

My ongoing Sunday morning trips to the flea market brought about a completely unrelated, but amazing chain of events for me to cherish.

The flea market is a hive of activity. Vendors of all kinds hawk their wares to a crowd of regular Sunday shoppers who are bargain hunters and novelty seekers. This ebbs and flows with the seasons and the weather. It was here that I realized indeed one man's junk can be another man's treasure.

I also discovered that it was the perfect place for serendipitous encounters and unexpected reunions with long lost family and friends. On one such occasion, I had the opportunity to update a retired teacher, once neighbour, on a former junior high school student. She was pleased to hear that my son was enjoying life in Japan.

On another visit, a fair-haired, bespectacled woman at a display table called out my name. I did a double take and recognized she was my younger cousin and the daughter of my favourite aunt. We had a lot of catching up to do so Carol offered a date and time to meet at her mom's home in our old neighbourhood.

Bringing cookies to the home that had meant so much to me growing up was an emotional moment. I recalled seeing my Aunt Kay and Uncle Cleve in their yard. They were never too busy to say hello and tell a tale or two. When Carol opened her mom's kitchen door, it was like turning the clock back to my childhood.

There was my petite Aunt Kay, calling out my name as she closed in to give me a hug. Her hair was short and salt and pepper in color. I was captivated at the sight of her dressed in a pink, blue, and white plaid button-up shirt and black pants. Carol had told me that her mom was approaching ninety-nine and was happy to live out her days in her own home.

Her children supported her wish with daily care and multiple phone calls. It was obvious that Aunt Kay's body had aged, but on that day, as we walked together to her cozy living room, it was clear that her recall and great sense of humour were intact. After we were seated, I handed her my cookies tied with pink ribbons, and basked in her giddiness.

Aunt Kay and I sat close together on her comfy sofa with Carol sitting close by. We took turns sharing our stories of the old days; at times we doubled over in laughter. There were also sad moments, feeling the loss of my mom and dad and her beloved husband.

Uncle Cleve was my dad's oldest brother. He was good-natured and always ready to lend a helping hand. I shared with her the day that he came to replace our kitchen floor. As I handed him a floor tile, he told little me, "It's important for the first tile to be in the centre of the room."

My aunt brought me back to the present when I heard her say, "I loved your mother; she was a beautiful woman and there for me when I needed her." This was an emotional moment for us both. Taking a breath, we continued our trip down memory lane as she told me that my mother and father never failed to visit every Christmas Eve. It was then I told her she had always been my favourite aunt. Her head was nodding as she patted my knee, showing how much this meant to her.

A few weeks later I returned with my youngest sister, Holly. I brought some old black and white photos of my mom and dad to give to her.

Aunt Kay studied the photo of my teenage mom holding a puppy in her arms. She repeated how much she loved and missed her. It was then I told her my mom loved her too! She savoured this as her eyes filled with tears.

My sweet sister enjoyed hearing the stories of long ago. She took a photo of me planting a kiss on my aunt's cheek, and I captured a precious photo of her delivering a big hug. We would cherish these reminders of our visit.

The following Sunday, I decided to bring some cookies to the flea market for Carol and her mom. After searching up and down the aisles, I had to accept she was not there. I got a glance from a familiar vendor, rather than her usual friendly smile. This was cause for concern. She was slightly built and soft-spoken, almost invisible among the more boisterous cohorts, but she had always been engaging.

When it was time to leave, I started for the door then stopped in my tracks. I felt the urge to go back to that vendor. I began thinking that she might depend on this income and a purchase could cheer her up. When I arrived at her table, she was talking with a potential customer but didn't make the sale.

When the man left, I shifted gears and rather than go through her inventory, I quickly stepped up and said I had something for her. She looked puzzled. I held up the package of cookies, tied with yellow curly ribbon saying, "I hope you'll enjoy them." Of course, mindful of allergies, I told her of the peanut butter content adding, "I don't want to kill you with kindness." I was hoping my humour would get an entertaining reaction.

Instead, this woman became teary-eyed and put her head down. Recovering, she looked at me and said that she was not allergic to peanuts. She reached out mechanically for the cookies and held them close. This woman let out a sigh and told me that her week had been a nightmare and she had barely made it to the flea market. Then, quietly she asked why I was giving her cookies. I told her it was a thank you for giving me a smile every Sunday.

I was surprised when she asked if she could hug me, and I welcomed it. She carefully set the cookies down, stepped away from her table, and put her arms around me, holding on tightly. She felt frail and vulnerable. As we embraced, she thanked me for my cookies and told me I had no idea what my act of kindness meant to her. I sensed she had been nearing her breaking point.

This virtual stranger did not choose to share her torment or hardship with me, and I did not ask any questions. Instead, we both basked in the moment, each comforted by the other. I assured her there would be better days ahead.

During a visit with my daughter in Alberta, I got the sad news that my Aunt Kay had passed on. It was just before her 100th birthday. I felt sad but also blessed having reconnected with her and for the precious time we shared.

During our last time together, she told me my Uncle Cleve was the only man she had ever loved. I felt peace with the thought that she had reunited with him. My heart went out to her children and her grandchildren. I knew they were facing many days and nights of sorrow.

I think life's gifts come in many forms. One such gift is coping with loss. When the grip of sadness begins to loosen, joy finds its way back to us to enjoy fond memories.

Chapter 6:
Just What I Needed

I was back in Calgary spending quality time with Amanda, my son-in-law, Mark, and my delightful grandchildren, Devon, Logan, and Clara. It was during this visit that I met an endearing little boy named Alex. He attended elementary school with my grandsons and was coming over after school for a playdate.

I was introduced by my grandchildren as if I were a celebrity. He seemed shy, as he quietly removed his backpack, coat, and shoes. Alex placed them with his lunch box at the foot of the stairs, close to the door. Then we all went off to the kitchen for a snack.

Shouts of "Hooray!" erupted as my grandchildren began to feast on my homemade cookies while downing tall glasses of refreshing cold milk. They chattered and giggled with chocolate-stained, milky moustaches. Alex passed on the cookies, saying he had brought his own snack. When everyone was finished, they disappeared up the stairs to the playroom for fun and games.

The doorbell rang hours later, and it was time for goodbyes. Alex's dad had arrived. I resisted my urge to give this shy boy a hug and hoped to see more of him.

During another one of my visits, we quickly ran out of the cookies I had brought. The day had come when my grandchildren would finally participate in the making of a new batch. Clara's job was to carefully pour in beaten eggs and vanilla. Devon and Logan took care of the dry ingredients. They all took turns stirring the cookie batter until the consistency was just right.

Spoonful's of batter were ready to be rolled into balls and placed on a cookie sheet. Initially, there were some gigantic balls needing to be downsized, and overzealous pressing with a wet fork, but my little apprentice bakers soon mastered the shaping process. Five chocolate chips were added to each cookie. I had them count to number five on one hand.

Over the years my cookies had come up from time-to-time in family conversations. Two amusing opinions concerned the ideal size and the number of chocolate chips on each. For the most part, the consensus was that the size was not as important as the number of chocolate chips. My grandchildren definitely adhered to the more chocolate chips the better school of thought. On that day they did get to put extra chips on some of their cookies.

When everyone was satisfied with their creations, the cookies were placed in the oven to bake. As my grandchildren and I cleaned up, my daughter announced that Alex would be coming over every school morning and afternoon for a few weeks.

Sure enough, the next day, Alex arrived with his mom and all the children were thrilled. It was great to see him again. As I write, I cannot help but feel the warmth of what transpired over the weeks ahead.

Since birth, my grandchildren had enjoyed my cuddles, head scratches, and back rubs. As time went by, they began to ask me to massage their arms and legs. My first experience with therapeutic touch was when their momma studied massage therapy and used me as her guinea pig. I learned about techniques of touch to calm, relax, and create connection.

One afternoon, I announced it was time for head scratches and mini massages. Alex watched curiously as my grandchildren lined up to wait their turn. His eyes widened when he saw how much they enjoyed the experience. First came Devon; he kept his eyes closed as if asleep. Next came Logan; his eyes were open, looking spacey and relaxed.

I then asked Alex if he too would like a turn. Despite his shyness, he immediately nodded yes and got in line. Clara loved her time, which she spent giggling. Then it was Alex's turn. He sat on the edge of the sofa as I gently began to massage his shoulders. I then asked, "So Alex, what do you think?" His response was, "I think I have to go and play with Legos." He stood up and off he went. This indeed prompted a chuckle from me.

Another pleasant surprise happened when Alex joined the cookie making team. He gave it his best. He enjoyed measuring and stirring with the others, and also learned a taste tester's job was important. It could involve eating more than one cookie. I called it 'quality' control, showing a thumb's up or down reaction. His mom had warned us that having Alex try new food could result in a quick getaway. I captured a photo of his chocolatey, milky grin along with the others as he devoured two of the cookies that he helped make. He gave an enthusiastic thumbs up! From that day on, Alex would call me Nanny-Ellen.

As my departure neared, I decided to bake a batch of cookies that could be stored in the freezer. This secret cookie stash delighted my daughter. I was leaving with amazing memories of the precious time I spent with my grandchildren and the new kid on the block. I even got the hug from Alex that I had been waiting for.

After a few weeks back home, I received an emotional phone call from Amanda. She told me that she had found Alex sitting on the bottom step near the door with his head in his hands. He had removed himself from after-school playtime with the children.

When she asked him what was wrong, he remained silent. Amanda tried everything within her power to lift his spirits. The only response she got was when he raised his head and showed his sad teary eyes. It broke her heart to see him like this and she wasn't sure what to do next. Then, she got a great idea.

My daughter remembered the stash of cookies stowed in her freezer, just waiting for the right time. She whispered the surprise into Alex's ear. His response was immediate, his tears receded like an ocean tide, and he headed for the kitchen.

Amanda returned from the basement and found him patiently perched on one of the high stools at the kitchen island. She opened the cookie container and placed it in front of him. Alex picked two cookies for her to warm up. When he finished his last bite, she asked him to go upstairs and tell Devon, Logan, and Clara to come down.

From the excited way Alex ran up the stairs, Amanda thought he would boast he had two of Nanny-Ellen's cookies. They came into the kitchen shocked to see the cookies and glasses of milk waiting for them. It was obvious that Alex wanted them to be surprised, just like he had been.

In the evening, Amanda called Alex's mom to tell her what had happened that day. She responded that her son tended to become very distraught when he got hungry.

The following day Alex's mom had something special to tell. She said that every night, when her son is tucked into bed, he shares what is in his head and heart before going off to sleep. He told his parents that Nanny-Ellen's cookies were just what he needed.

Chapter 7:
Most Eventful
Car Recall Experience

I bought a used Volkswagen hatchback with low mileage and a history of only one owner. Its interior was pristine. I liked its coat of grey and that its trunk was spacious and welcomed my purchases, large and small. This car became my trusted best friend in all kinds of weather. As with any friendship, I wanted to give it the care and attention it deserved.

Andrew, a car-savvy new acquaintance of mine, brought my attention to some small rust spots on my car. He warned me they would soon get worse. Then he instantly checked out the on-line information pertaining to my car by using his trusty tablet device. It was then he confirmed a recall had been issued.

I appreciated Andrew's keen eye and sound advice to act quickly. My cookies were no stranger to him, and I would make sure he got an abundance to munch on.

I called a nearby dealership and was told I would have to fill out some forms which could be done conveniently from my home computer. It was most impressive to be given an early morning appointment a few days later. Upon my arrival, a polite young man took my name and directed me to a small seating area. Shortly afterward, a young lady with a clip board, greeted me saying, "I'm Jamie-Rae and

I'll be inspecting your vehicle today." I led the way to my car.

She looked up at the blue sky and commented that it was going to be a good day. Then she got down to business. I pointed out three rust concerns around the wheel wells. She took a close look and recorded them. Jamie-Rae then told me she would do a more thorough inspection and recommended I go back inside where I would be more comfortable. She was an attractive, personable young woman who struck me as a competent professional.

I returned and settled into the same seat I had previously occupied. At times like these, I was grateful for my bag with water and crossword puzzles. Just when it seemed that Jamie-Rae was taking longer than I expected, she appeared, voicing there were several other concerns. She began to thumb through the pages on her clipboard. Feeling some unease, I hoped there would be no out-of-pocket costs for me to deal with.

Jamie-Rae began with her discovery of other rust issues around the trunk. My impending mental hurricane of concern evaporated with her words of, "I am happy to tell you all of these issues are covered by the recall."

This dedicated manager explained everything thoroughly to me. She then asked if I had any questions. My response was that I had two important questions. First, I asked if she was allergic to peanuts. Her face took on a curious expression as she told me that peanut butter was a favorite of hers. Without skipping a beat, I asked my second question to find out if she liked chocolate. Her answer was no, then enthusiastically she said, "I love chocolate!"

With those answers, I reached into my canvas bag, pulled out my homemade cookies and gave them to her. She excitedly accepted the colorful spiralled ribbon-tied package and thanked me. Then she asked, "Do I have to share?" Her comeback was hilarious. My answer matched her wit when I said, "You're the boss." We both giggled like young schoolgirls.

I told Jamie-Rae that my mom encouraged me to show my appreciation to those who were kind and helpful. She said that her mom was exactly the same. We then got back to business. After signing some papers, it was time for me to leave. With a smile and a handshake, we wished each other a great day ahead.

Back in my car, I realized that I was still holding her fancy pen. The building was only steps away, so off I went to return it. I told the receptionist that I needed to briefly see Jamie-Rae again, and within minutes out she came, flashing that great big smile of hers.

Our extra time together was totally gratifying. I apologized for the interruption and said, "Jamie-Rae, my mom not only instilled in me the importance of showing gratitude, she also taught me not to steal." I then handed her the silver pen with the company's crest on it. She chuckled and instinctively gave me a hug while saying, "I'm glad you returned."

This wonderful woman said that I had brightened her day and she wanted to pay it forward. Jamie-Rae confided that baking was not really her thing and that she would find her own way to shine light on someone's day. Jamie-Rae then graciously placed the pen back in the palm of my hand and said, "This is a start."

... and That's the Way My Cookies Crumble

Chapter 8:
My Worldly Children and International Bonding

It was my purpose in life to be there for my children. I encouraged them to find gratification in what they did and helped them to reach for their dreams. It was my hope for them to become happy, fulfilled adults. As I look back on those years we spent together, I realize how much they influenced me.

Amanda chose to enter French Immersion in her first year of junior high school. What she didn't know at the time was the following year she would be given an opportunity to host a student from France. She welcomed this as an ideal opportunity to take advantage of.

The application process involved responding to questionnaires focused on compatibility. My daughter, son, and I agreed on a male approximately sixteen years old, sincere, open-minded, and with a good sense of humour. When it came to interests, we chose art, music, and the martial arts.

Amanda began to correspond with the young man who the ASSE International Student Exchange Program had matched her with. Then, in early summer, there we were at the arrivals gate of our International Airport, holding up high a welcome sign to greet Yann Bréhin. We expected a large group of students, so with his photo in hand, we waited to pick him out of the crowd. It was easier than we had expected because he was as tall as a giraffe, towering over the others.

I saw that Yann did not let his nervousness interfere with settling into his homestay. It started with a family campout by the sea in our rugged Nova Scotian landscape of Parrsboro. We got to know more about each other while sitting around a campfire under the stars. There, Yann told us that his father had helped him choose our country and province because the ocean would remind him of home.

Another kind of campout was planned knowing that he was a black belt in judo. Our French student was invited to attend the Karate Summer Camp East with its indoor and outdoor beach training. There he met many people from all over our Maritime provinces and was welcomed into the homes of our Acadian French karate friends. Many wonderful memories were made as he became acquainted with our style of karate and shared some of his judo skills.

It was a pleasure to show our city to Yann. The Halifax Museum of Natural History and Maritime Museum of the Atlantic fascinated him, along with our Halifax Citadel Natural Historic Site. This gave him a spectacular panoramic view of our city and harbour. He also enjoyed strolling through the village that is home to our pride and joy, the Peggy's Cove lighthouse. Yann enjoyed the ocean view and the Sou'Wester Gift Shop. We then sat in its restaurant and filled our bellies with a tasty lobster dinner.

We spent busy times together and learned that Yann was fun to be with, both inside and outside our home. He even offered to help with chores ranging from kitchen clean up to mowing the lawn.

Our goodbye at summer's end was emotional. It was then we learned 'adieu' means you will never meet again in this world, while 'au revoir' means till we meet again. As Yann entered the airport check-in area, he turned and said, "au revoir."

A feeling of emptiness lingered without Yann's presence. Then an abundance of letters began to flow back and forth as we shared the goings-on in our lives. All of his letters remain safely stowed by me. It was sweet to hear Yann say that he had kept all our letters.

To our delight, he returned the following summer. Then the year after that, he travelled with his father, Jean-Claude, who was attending a seminar in our city. We showed him the sights his son had come to love. He agreed with me that it was wonderfully satisfying that our children had an extraordinary friendship.

Amanda and Marc accepted an invitation to visit Yann's home in France in the summer of 1996. Yann and his dad met them in Paris and immediately they drove to Brittany in northwestern France. When they arrived,, Yann's mom, Chantal, his older sister, Stephanie, and brothers, Patrick and Laurent welcomed them.

Their awesome time unfolded beginning with the medieval architecture of the town Yann had grown up in and the making of new friends. My children returned home with lots of photos and stories of their adventure.

*****

Both my son and daughter decided to study abroad. Amanda was the first to leave. Her brother was happy for her and teased that in her absence he would reclaim his 'only child' status. Yann's father and mother were teachers which was an encouragement for Amanda to return to Yann's family home. There she spent what would have been her grade 11 (1997-1998) in their school system.

Amanda excelled in her studies, made friendships and valued how much she learned about herself. There was always something new to discover and write home about. Class trips included travel to Wales and England's Stonehenge. Family vacations took her to Mont Saint-Michel and the French Alps, among other places.

Following high school, my daughter chose a career related to healthcare. She graduated from the Canadian College of Natural Medicine in 2001 as a Registered Massage Therapist. Her goal was to provide therapeutic care and give comfort to those in need.

At a young age, my son was fascinated with the Japanese culture. During his last year of high school, he met and befriended a student from Saitama, Japan. Aiko had come to Canada to improve her English language skills. They met at Sir John A MacDonald High School and an immediate friendship blossomed; they were interested in each other's country. Aiko's visits to our home were frequent and fun; this included spending Christmas together. We had a huge celebration when we became her alternate host family. Our connection would last a lifetime.

Marc went on to study at our local Saint Mary's University. In 1999, he earned a one-year full scholarship to attend a university in Halifax's sister city of Hakodate in

Hokkaido, Japan. Since the 1990s, Halifax has been sending a Christmas tree every year to Hakodate as a symbol of friendship. Marc was thrilled to be present at a tree lighting ceremony.

While in Japan, he travelled to Kumamoto in the southern Kyushu region. He visited ancient temples and shrines, felt the comfort of its world-famous hot springs, and admired the beauty of its magnificent mountains. Then my son's childhood wish finally came true. He felt privileged to be within the walls of the Sohonbu World Headquarters dojo.

Upon finishing his studies in Hakodate, he returned home eager to complete his Bachelor of Arts degree in Asian Studies. He then headed back to Japan in 2001, assuming the position of an Assistant Language Teacher in the Kumamoto school system. This allowed him to interact with many students, explore most of Japan, hone his karate skills, and study Shodo, the art of Japanese calligraphy.

Marc and Amanda shared with each other their personal experiences of living abroad. This included their handling of missing home, fun times and, times when they needed to dig deep to cope with the challenges of cultural immersion. An amusing memory stays with me of Marc sending home a message to his sister written in Japanese; he offered to translate. Amanda replied to him in French. My son's response was short and in English. It read, Good One!

In 2002, my daughter and I travelled to the other side of the world to spend time with Marc. Our trip of a lifetime started with reunion hugs in Narita Airport. Immediately following, we met Nakayama Sensei. He and his family showered us with legendary Japanese hospitality. As his guests, we were taken to historic sites near and far. One day culminated on the deck of a high-rise downtown building. Nakayama Sensei, kindly treated us to a magnificent daytime view and, following our meal, a dazzling nighttime view of Japan's famous Tokyo city. When it was time for good-byes, we extended our sincere appreciation to the Nakayama family.

With vim and vigor, we boarded a train that would take us to meet Aiko's parents in Saitama. Her beautiful mom, Takako, and her charming dad, Kozo, were at the train station waiting for our arrival. With hearts overflowing, we bowed to one another. It felt dreamlike to be sitting together in the Inoue's cozy kitchen. Aiko joined us by telephone. It was an irony that she was not with us. Instead, she was in Canada continuing her studies. We promised to gather together again with Aiko present.

Takako and Kozo took us on a tour which included the world-famous Tosho-gu shrine in Nikko. There, we bowed and cleansed before entering to show respect. I was astonished to see the three wise monkeys of 'hear no evil, speak no evil, see no evil' and learn they had originated from that location. The monkeys were colourfully depicted in bas-relief panels on the wall of the Oumaya, or Sacred Horse Stable, at the shrine. The vast complex of meticulously kept grounds and age old structures were mystical to behold.

We then went on to enjoy an overnight stay at the Kinugawa Hotsprings Sanraku Hotel. It was perched high above the gushing Kinugawa River. Immediately upon entering the hotel, we were welcomed by a woman wearing a traditional Japanese kimono. She escorted us to a table and brought tea. In our room, Amanda and I donned the waiting

Japanese ukatas (a casual version of the kimono). After a delicious meal of traditional sushi, we were invited to indulge in the ever-popular traditional Japanese *onsen*, a hot spring-fed bath. It would be the first time for us; Marc highly recommended it.

The guys went off to their onsen location while Aiko's mom led us to ours. I hesitated for a moment before removing my ukata and undergarments and then placed them in a cupboard that offered me a small towel. Takako took us to where we would prepare. A convenient low counter top held toiletries and wooden buckets filled with water. We sat low on 3-legged wooden stools while washing and rinsing our bodies. Once ready, we were shown several hot spring-fed pools. As if by enchantment, mist hovered above one with its water seemingly spilling out onto what lay below. A riveting view of the glorious mountainous sights was delivered by a large floor-to-ceiling window. Takako then took us to a nearby outdoor onsen. We climbed into the tub and blissfully relaxed in its soothing waters. I marvelled at how it made my inhibitions melt away.

We reunited with Kozo and Marc for a glass of cold beer and some delicious ginger root pickles that we ate with chopsticks. At twilight time, we took a stroll, enjoying the refreshing evening air. We basked in these precious moments shared. At bedtime, Amanda and I quickly drifted off to sleep, still feeling the beneficial effects of the *onsen*.

Before leaving this area, Takako and Kozo had another wonderful surprise. We boarded a gondola that took us upwards to leisurely explore the surroundings of a mountain while listening to enchanting, traditional Japanese music. I felt euphoric with the spectacular view on our way back down. I felt as if I had been given a glimpse of Heaven.

Our last night with Aiko's parents was one of ease, for we knew we would be together again.

Our next stop was a two-night sleepover in a temple. We were thrilled to be in the ancient city of Kyoto. It had been Japan's capital for more than 1000 years before the seat of government moved to Tokyo. Once again, we were given ukatas to wear. We slept on tatami mats which we rolled up the following morning. Our breakfast was served in an adjoining room and while seated at the low table, an open sliding door revealed a quaint garden.

I was very surprised to witness such an abundance of bicycles everywhere I looked. It was interesting to see one bicycle with a small child sitting in a basket in front of the handlebars while presumably the father was peddling. The mother was standing behind him on foot pegs with her hands resting on his shoulders. I saw they were totally at ease while moving perfectly balanced along the crowded street. I took many photos of Kyoto's beauty, including the incredible awe-inspiring Golden Pavilion; its image was mirrored flawlessly in the surrounding pond.

Our train route to Kumamoto allowed us to see many rice fields and the majestic Mount Fuji off in the distance. Marc was excited to show us his home away from home. He took us to the formidable Kumamoto Castle and Mount Aso, the largest active volcano in Japan. It is also among the largest in the world. Gazing into it was a thrill. Marc took me for a spin in his low to the ground, red two-seater Honda del Sol convertible. He timed it for me to experience the large, brilliant red sun vanish slowly into the horizon. It was spectacular.

The time had finally come for Amanda and me to meet Reika, the woman who had captured my son's heart. She was gorgeous, strong, and committed to always give her best. We also had the opportunity to visit with her mom. Michiyo's home in the nature-rich town of Oguni, surrounded by mountains, was enchanting. The meal she prepared for us was delicious. In the future it was my pleasure to meet Reika's older married sister, Hiromi Oba, who lives and works in Tokyo.

Amanda and I were grateful to meet those at Marc's workplace and his new friends who graciously invited us into their homes. While lying in bed in my son's cozy apartment on the last night of our visit, I knew our family time together had been much needed. It was most important and a huge relief for me to be able to visualize where my son was living and how he spent his days. Amanda, Marc and I would always look back on and hold dear the great times we shared exploring the country he dreamed of since he was a boy.

*****

The continued momentum of my adult children's lives brought about a significant change in my own. I woke up one day to an empty apartment. They had encouraged me to fill the space they left with international students. I took their advice, and it enriched my life in ways that I could never have imagined. I welcomed each student with open arms saying, "This is your room, and this is your home for as long as you want."

Yuriko Tanaka from Osaka, Japan found my room rental on a website. She had begun her studies in Ontario and arrived in Nova Scotia in 2003, to complete them. She received her Bachelor of Fine Arts in textiles from the Nova Scotia College of Art and Design one year later. Together we celebrated her well-deserved achievement. Her parents arrived from Japan to see her art exhibit, 'Influence'. Kayoko, her mom, and Seiji, her dad, were a pleasure to be with.

There was a day when Yuriko needed a few hours to attend to business, so I decided to take her parents to picturesque Peggy's Cove. We communicated using a combination of familiar words and body language. Seiji would offer his hand to help me navigate the rocky terrain, and Kayoko's eyes and smile conveyed that she was having a great time. It felt like a family day to me. Returning to my place, we drank coffee, ate cookies, and waited for Yuriko to come home. She and I both missed her parents when they returned to Osaka.

Most of Yuriko's time in Canada had been focused on her studies. She made an important decision to extend her stay to experience more of the Canadian lifestyle. I helped with her Permanent Residency application. She found a job in a downtown tailor shop and made the most of her free time. We enjoyed our conversations while feasting on her delicious homemade gyosa (dumplings) and my peanut butter chocolate chip cookies. We lived in harmony; influenced by each other, made us stronger. When Yuriko told me that I was her *shinyu*, best friend, I was deeply touched and told her that we indeed had a very special connection. I then told her she was my shinyu.

In July of 2006, my daughter and her fiancé, Mark, were married in a local nearby church. Yann arrived from France to attend their wedding and promised to join us in Japan in October where Marc and Reika would wed in a traditional Shinto Shrine. My children had found their life partners.

Yann stayed at my apartment with me for the remainder of his time spent in Canada. He and Yuriko got to know one another, and I sensed a spark between them. These two international students from different countries and backgrounds fell in love. The future would bring another wedding. I would be asked to be their witness at their civil marriage ceremony taking place in Brittany in 2009. It would be a time for Yuriko's mom and I to meet again, and join Yann's parents, family, and friends in celebration. In the years ahead, Yann and Yuriko would welcome two sons.

Just before Yuriko moved out into an apartment of her own in 2007 to be closer to her new job, she introduced me to Megumi. Her newfound friend had arrived from Tokyo to improve her English. Megumi Yamada moved into Yuriko's vacant room for a three-month stay and would return home at December's end. She relished the yellow, orange, and reds of Canada's autumn leaves and a Thanksgiving dinner at my table. At a class Halloween party, she wore the beautiful red kimono Aiko had given me as a gift. Megumi also got to celebrate her November thirtieth birthday and to experience the magic of a Canadian Christmas with Yuriko, Yann, and me.

Decorating the Christmas tree was playful for all. On Christmas Eve, I watched my dear international family hang the Christmas stockings I had made for them. They were as giddy as children to find them full the next morning, and to see the gifts Santa had left under the tree.

Megumi happily learned to make my peanut butter chocolate chip cookies. She married years later in Japan and had a daughter and a son. If they were peanut friendly, Megumi could make these cookies for her children. Having spent only a short time together, we cherish our ongoing precious friendship.

Mei-Feng Luo found me through the Saint Mary's University website. We met and within less than a week, she moved in. When I introduced her to my family and friends, I would jokingly open with, "Mei, was made in Taiwan." It got a lot of giggles. I told her that it had been common for boxes of popcorn to contain prizes labelled, made in Taiwan. Mei and I shared that our friendship indeed was a most valuable prize.

She had just finished a Bachelor of Commerce degree and was working on a Certificate in Business. I was very happy to attend her graduation ceremony. Mei spent many years studying in Nova Scotia, and also committed to volunteer work. When she said she wanted to make Canada her home, I immediately offered to help in any way I could. Mei first became a Permanent Resident of Canada and, five years later, we were celebrating her Canadian Citizenship.

It was a thrill for me to be invited to visit Mei's homeland. Upon reaching our destination, we stepped through an ornate red door, climbed a flight of stairs and entered the home of her mom, Yu-Mei Lu. It was wonderful to spend time with her and Mei's two sisters, Shiow-Lian, Mei-Lan, and her brother, Yin-Min. Their balcony looked out onto the narrow street below where every day an outdoor market would set up late morning and again in the early evening. When darkness fell, the marketplace would light up, so the hustle and bustle could continue unabated on the crowded street. Voices rang out from the vendors selling a variety of goods and food. Fresh meat and inner parts of animals hung on hooks while a variety of fish rested on ice. It was a sight to behold of oversized shapes and colors of various fruits both familiar and unfamiliar along with vegetables laying on tables, waiting to be purchased and enjoyed.

I was grateful for the opportunity to travel across the country. A sleepover with Mei in a Buddhist temple was an extraordinary experience. Yu-Mei Lu took us to visit many others which ranged in size and grandeur.

We used multiple trains, subways, and buses to reach distant areas. Otherwise, in Taipei, we rode bicycles and scooters which were perfect for getting around locally.

The Taipei 101 tower, once the tallest man-made structure in the world was impressive. I enjoyed the many other sights and sounds of Taipei's bustling city.

I felt safe on the back of Mei's scooter; she drove confidently. Making our way to a special place, we crossed a narrow two-laned bridge. My view of the water below and the blue sky above gave me a needed feeling of absolute serenity. Her mom's garden was located on a hillside. We hiked up an ill-defined path and there she was, working in her vegetable garden amid the bamboo trees.

Yu-Mei Lu took Mei and me on a lengthy bus ride to the area where she was born and grew up. There, I met some of her family. Then I was taken to where Confucius had once lived and taught for a time. I read that this ancient well-known Chinese philosopher, politician, and teacher was charming, selfless, and dedicated to people. He was indeed insightful to profess to not impose on others what you do not wish for yourself. I am forever grateful to have visited a place where he had been.

Towards the end of my Taiwan adventure, I met Ren-Wei, a school friend of Mei's. I felt an instant connection. She invited Mei and me to travel with her by train to bathe in Yilin County's famous hot springs and view its splendid cascading waterfalls.

Days after that, we would be guests at another friend's wedding party. This married couple changed outfits several times. My favourite was that of a Prince and Princess. They made their way into the spacious dining room in a bird cage shaped carriage. Then Maroon 5's North American song, 'Sugar' began to play. This triggered me seeing their popular wedding-crashing video. I was completely swept away by this unforgettable romantic night.

Ren-Wei reminded me of my early days. She had no plans to see the world. I wanted to inspire her as I had been by others, so I invited her to come to Canada. She beamed and promised to think about it.

Shortly after returning to Canada, Mei and I were elated to receive her message that she was coming in 2020. Sadly, a global pandemic squashed this. We would wait patiently, determined that plans will be made when it is safe once again to travel.

I highly recommend to those who are entertaining the thought of opening their home to an international student, to act on it.

Chapter 9:
Nanny-Ellen's Cookie Fan Club

I am blessed to have five fantastic grandchildren. Like their parents, they contribute greatly to my ongoing personal growth. Their curiosity, and eagerness to take on new challenges, like sport, dance, playing a musical instrument and more is delightful for me to witness.

My first grandchild, Reina, was born 2009 in Japan to Marc and Reika. She was brown eyed and had an abundance of dark brown hair. We met the following year in Kumamoto. There she gifted me an unforgettable memory. As we strolled alongside a cement wall, she bolted ahead then stopped and looked back at me as if to say, "Are you coming?" I accepted her challenge, caught up, and ran passed her. Then I stopped and, facing the wall, spread my hands on it. Reina saw this, picked up her pace and whisked by me. To my absolute surprise, she mimicked what I had done but did not wait for me to catch up, for she was determined to win the race. The end of the wall signalled the end of our game and her victory.

Sadly, distance prevented in-person play dates but, thanks to technology, we got to see and hear each other on screen. I loved the videos that captured my granddaughter's playfulness, as well as her karate classes, school events, and dance recitals. Reina wisely focuses on her studies and gets the best results to enhance her future. My granddaughter is beautiful inside and out. I believe her positive attitude and making good choices will bring her a happy and fulfilling life.

My grandson, Devon, was born 2010 in Alberta to Amanda and Mark. He was blue eyed with a sprinkle of blonde hair. We share being born in a Year of the Tiger. At age three, Devon's babysitter, Tessa Andrews, noticed his little Milky Way t-shirt and explained what it was. His curiosity prompted her to tell him about the planets. He was fascinated, wanting to hear more and see lots of visuals. On one of my visits, Devon asked me to make my cookies for him to share with Tessa. Their chemistry was a sight to behold. In pre-school, the teachers marvelled at his accurate knowledge and drawings of all the planets. When Devon was six, he experienced the thrill of a lifetime as one of his schoolteachers made it possible for him to meet his hero, astronaut Chris Hadfield.

At a young age, my grandson told me that he would work on a way for me to celebrate my 150th birthday. With his incredible mind and persevering spirit, I am convinced he will do great things for mankind.

Logan, a brother to Devon, arrived in 2012. He had blue eyes and also had to wait for his hair to grow. As it grew, it was blonde and with a curl. From the start, he was a freethinker. I will never forget sitting with my daughter on her sundeck just a few hours before my flight home. Logan's five-year-old voice rang out from an upper window, "Nanny-Ellen, come up! I want to tell you something." Amanda called back, "Logan come down here and tell her." He responded, "Okay Momma but you're not gonna like it." He arrived hauling behind him a small travel bag on wheels; his favourite stuffy, Puppy, was strapped to it. He looked at me saying, "Nanny-Ellen, I'm going with you."

Then he looked tentatively at his momma. She put her hand on her chest and mournfully said, "Logan" He responded quickly saying, "It's okay Momma, you can come visit us."

My grandson is a kind-hearted soul, always helping others with his infinite understanding and patience. He is a natural entertainer as well. His facial expressions and character mimicking dialogues bring laughter to many. I believe that he will come to be recognized and valued as a genuine humanitarian and a very good friend to have.

Then came my grandson, Kenshi, born 2014, in Japan. Reina's little brother had a twinkle in his eyes and was quite big at birth. Unlike his sister, he had only a hint of light brown hair on the top of his head. The colour of his eyes would eventually darken to match the growth of his slightly curly, dark brown hair. Kenshi personifies the Japanese term of genki (energetic, full of spirit). He and his cousin, Logan, have remarkable similar facial features, as well as similar personalities and mannerisms.

As my grandson grew, we met on screen and played games such as peek-a-boo. Having precious video play dates, warmed my heart. Kenshi began to hold up huge live insects for me to see. He was enthralled with them. From the other side of the world, I enjoyed seeing his hilarious playtimes with his older sister, Reina. Sadly, life circumstances have ongoing kept us apart. This includes the 2016 earthquakes and the 2020 pandemic. I look forward to meeting my grandson, Kenshi in person and sharing fun times.

Clara my fifth grandchild, was born in 2015. Like her brothers, she was pretty much bald at birth. Around two, her silky blonde locks began to grow and complimented her blue eyes. My daughter decided early on that her name would be Clara. When I met her in the hospital, a few hours after her birth, Amanda gifted me the surprise that Clara's second name was Marie, the same as mine.

My granddaughter is a quick learner. Her interests and energy are a sight to behold. This girl has a lot of love to give. Clara is an animated communicator, and she often delivers plenty of 'pleases' and 'thankyous'. I have felt the joy and have seen the same results in others, from the many compliments she gives. Like her beautiful cousin Reina, she too loves ballet. They both look gorgeous with their hair up while dressed in their dance outfits.

A common thread among my grandchildren is their artistic talent and creative imagination. I treasure being a part of their world to bring life to their stuffed animals, be it Devon's Baby Monkey, Logan's Puppy, or Clara's Lambie. Reina and Kenshi were always amused by my animated puppets of Tiger, Hopper the Rabbit, and Mr. Owl who was a hoot as he flew about during our facetimes together.

I am proud of each and everyone of my grandchildren. I have taken delight in seeing their faces light up with their achievements, big and small. For instance, when their last puzzle piece is snapped into place, or the last Lego is connected. They would often identify what they had done as epic and basked in what they had achieved.

I have also seen them when their creations would go sideways or while coping with a bad day. These disappointments could bring heartache and a flood of tears.

Their amazing resilience and willpower to not give up is fueled by their constant desire to invite fun, friendships and newness into their lives. They inspire me.

My grandchildren are the sunshine in my life. It totally warms my heart that each and every one of them is an enthusiastic fan of my cookies.

Chapter 10:
Karate Influence and Growth

I never intended to study the martial arts and was unaware that the practice of Chito-Ryu Karate Do could, at any age, profoundly change one's life both mentally and physically.

The hardship of my fair-haired, green eyed little boy would set an important path for both of us. As a child, like me Marc was quiet and submissive. This made him a target for school bullies. What started out as teasing and pranks, turned into full-blown physical aggression.

When I had seen Anton at school functions, he was a charming little boy. He fooled a lot of people. When my son told me Anton constantly took his belongings, I approached his teacher and asked her to keep a watchful eye and intervene when needed.

My son's spirit was waning. I decided to meet him after school, so we could walk home together. As I rounded the school building, the children were spilling out of its doors. I witnessed my son's nightmare for the first time. Anton came up from behind and shoved him to the ground. I ran over and told him in a controlled voice that it was a mean thing to do. Surprise flickered in his eyes before turning to slyness as he blurted out, "I didn't hurt him." Then off he went. I feared my son was close to his breaking point and scheduled a talk with the principal. It was shocking to hear him tell me that Anton had been on his radar screen for a while, and that he had done all he could.

In the 80s, the Yellow Page section of the local telephone book provided business names and contact information. Starting with the letter A, I looked for a place where my ten-year-old son could learn to defend himself. At the other end of the line, a male voice said, "This is the Atlantic Karate Club, what can we do for you?"

After hearing Marc's situation, he said, "Our style of karate is called Chito-Ryu Karate Do and its headquarters is in Kumamoto, Japan. We will teach your son that fighting is not the answer to solving problems." He went on to say that taking traditional karate classes instills awareness and self-discovery. He added that it teaches self-defence is to be used only when necessary and finished with, "Why not bring your son in to watch or join in a class if he wants." I thanked him and relief swept over me.

The following Saturday we arrived at a Community School building to check out the youth class. The AKC was located at its far end. We climbed two flights of stairs to reach our destination. Five powerful words were present above the closed double doors: Character, Sincerity, Self-Control, Etiquette and Effort

Seeing multiple pairs of assorted footwear outside these doors, we removed ours and entered. In front of us was a small desk and chair. To our right were the male and female changing rooms, and to our left was a wide-open space with windows on three sides.

Ahead, in clear view, we saw a few free-standing full-length mirrors. Centered above them was a framed photo of an older Japanese gentleman and beneath it was one of a younger man. Both men wore a white uniform, (*gi*) with a red crest on the left breast side. My son and I would come to learn that the older man was Okinawan Master, Dr. Tsuyoshi Chitose, the founder of Chito-Ryu Karate Do in Kumamoto, Japan. The younger man was his son who was continuing the teachings of his father, who had passed on. He is known throughout the world as Soke.

We saw a group ranging in age from eight to twelve. Sensei Peter Miller greeted us and invited Marc to join his class. He then turned and bowed before entering the dojo training area. It felt good to see my son mimic him. When the sensei walked towards the mirrors and said line up, the reaction was immediate. His students moved quickly to form several rows of four across. The space between each student was an arm's length. This discipline was impressive. Marc took his place in the back row.

My son was eager to wear a *gi* and continue taking classes. One day, as I watched him training, the dojo door swung open. I turned and stared at a familiar face. "What are you doing here?" we both exclaimed. It was a cousin I had not seen in a few years. I answered first, telling her my son had started karate lessons. Allison, who was eleven years my junior, did not skip a beat saying, "I volunteer here as a bookkeeper and my boyfriend, Chris, is in karate."

Our chance meeting was an opportunity to catch up. I told her I had fond childhood memories of my favourite Uncle Buddy's unexpected visits to my childhood home. Her dad, a quiet man, would take my mom and us kids out on fun drives, even a swim or two at a lake. She said he always had a special place in his heart for his older sister, my mom.

I pointed Marc out to Allison. She had not seen him since he was an infant. As we watched him, I felt joy knowing that my ten-year-old son was on a path to a happier future. This was confirmed over the coming months; his confidence was increasing, and his schoolwork was improving significantly.

*****

Four years later, Marc was thriving with karate as an essential part of his life. I, on the other hand, was at an all-time low.

My mom lost her valiant battle with cancer when she was sixty-two. This left me devastated and unable to handle my life. I was floating in my clothes, dropping to ninety-two pounds. Looking in the mirror one day, I could see that the light had gone out of my eyes. I felt like I was dying on the inside. This terrified me because my son and daughter relied on me.

One day, while cleaning out Marc's clothes closet, I found his first karate *gi* and decided to try it on. It was a Cinderella-like moment. I put on the pants, then slipped my arms through the jacket's sleeves and wrapped it around me. It fit. I was wearing it when my teenage son came home.

He did a double take and his eyes widened as he said, "Mom, you have to start karate." It had never occurred to me to do so. Upon reflection, I believe that deep down, I needed my son to say that. Pampering myself had never been a priority for me. Like my mom, I kept busy taking care of my husband and our children. Feeling the ongoing sting of losing her, I agonized over the fact that she had given away much of her life without a care for herself. I decided to try to not do that.

I asked my husband if he wanted to take a karate class with me and our son. It took some convincing from Marc and he finally agreed. After that class, he said it was not for him. I continued to attend with the mindset that I was doing it a bit for myself but mostly for my son; it gave us more quality time together. Marc was fourteen at the time and I was forty-two.

Together, we would climb the two flights of stairs to the dojo. In my weakened mental and physical state, I had to pause on the first landing. Seeing my son reach the top excited to train, prompted me to continue on up.

When we lined up for our class, I always felt nervous, so I positioned myself near the door. During workouts, feeling weary and with my face flushed, I wasn't sure if I could stay. The time came when Sensei Steven Gionet asked if I was feeling okay. With my response of, "I think so." he called a water break.

Sensei Gionet took me aside and said, "I've noticed you always line up near the door and during workouts tend to look in that direction." He told me to drink some water and see him after class. I listened intently to this sensei as he explained the concept of 'fight or flight'. He told me, when facing danger or difficult situations, we can decide to fight or take flight by running away. He assured me that feeling stressed and overwhelmed can come with trying something new. Sensei Gionet then prompted me to give my training more time and ended with, "Next class, I do not want to see you close to the door." This was a turning point for me. I began to concentrate more on my training and recognized that I was making some progress. My Tuesday and Thursday night karate classes were nurturing my self-esteem.

Approximately a year later, Chief Instructor Sensei Michael Delaney told me that it was time for me to move to his Monday and Wednesday night adult classes. He'd been informed I was ready.

Moving to a different schedule than Marc's meant I would have to drive to the dojo four nights a week. I was also timid about the change. I explained the travel situation to Sensei Delaney. He said he would make an exception, and allow Marc to attend his adult class and, if he met its requirements, he would be welcomed to continue.

Marc and I were happy that he proved he was capable, and we continued to train together. His relationship with Sensei Delaney grew strong. One night after a class, Sensei took Marc aside and asked if something was wrong. My son confided that a high school acquaintance had committed suicide.

Sensei consoled him. Then I heard him say, "Marc, I have something for you at my house." This meant I had to drive into the city, something I dreaded. I fought through my unease and asked Sensei to make sure he could see me in his rear-view mirror. When we arrived, his house was in darkness. Sensei got out of his car and told us to stay put. A light in his basement came on, accompanied by sounds of shifting and banging. Eventually, sensei reappeared, and we got out of the car.

Sensei Delaney wore a big grin as he approached us saying, "Marc, you passed your brown belt grading and I want to make it official." My son had been waiting for this news. Sensei Delaney then said to Marc, "I want you to have my brown belt." and handed it to him. In a state of disbelief, my son took it and thanked him. All the way home he kept saying, "I just can't believe this."

At the next class, Marc wore sensei's belt without a word to the others. After the workout, he told sensei he needed to talk. Sensei Delaney told him to come to his office and walked to the back of the dojo. There sensei sat cross-legged on the piled up mats, listening to Marc. Their meeting was brief. I hoped my son had found some peace of mind as I watched them head to the changing room.

On the drive home, Marc said he had thanked Sensei Delaney again and promised him he would take care of his brown belt until the day came for him to return it. Dumbfoundedly, he repeated Sensei Delaney's exact words at their meeting, "This belt is now yours, not mine." Marc said he then stood up and began walking away. Marc told me, upon catching up with him, he heard him say, "If my belt could talk, it would have a lot of interesting stories for people to hear"

*****

Marc was excited to learn his scholarship was confirmed to study at a university in northern Japan. I was thrilled for him, and then the reality set in that we wouldn't be attending karate classes together for a whole year. My classmates noticed that this hit me hard and were there to lift my spirits. One night, Sensei Delaney invited me to go along with some others for sushi in the city. I thanked him but had to decline and watched them all drive off.

While walking to my car, I saw Gary Sabean. I admired the dedication of this young black belt who strived for perfection. I asked if he was going for sushi. He said he had biked to class and would be heading home. Then, I made him an offer I hoped he wouldn't refuse. I asked if he wanted to put his bike in my car so we could join the others for sushi. There was a catch. I told him that he would have to drive. I confessed my fear of city driving and added, "I don't share this with just anyone." He accepted my offer and as he stowed his bike, he said, "Ellen, your secret is safe with me. God Love Yah." Gary's great sense of humour was enjoyed during the meal, and I got my first chopstick lesson.

Sensei Delaney was very intuitive. His ability to connect with and inspire each student was extraordinary. It became a common occurrence that, after a class, we changed into our street clothes and joined sensei as he sat at the front desk. He would share his vast knowledge of Chito-Ryu Karate-Do philosophy.

This time together reminded us to never doubt that we could achieve our goals in life. Sensei Delaney also had a great sense of humour. When he decided our chat time was over, he would then lean back in his chair, put his hands behind his head and scan his audience. Hearing him say, "You don't have to go home, but you can't stay here." never got old. From time-to-time, some of us would treat sensei to miso soup or a dessert at a coffee shop.

Marc and I were fortunate to get to know San Fung, Mitchell German, and Gary Sabean. These young black belts were true to their traditional training and also participated in competitions in and out of our province of Nova Scotia. As the years passed, they would go on to compete successfully worldwide.

They were focused and fearless. With sincere hearts, determination, and commitment to their extra training, they earned not only gold medals but also the respect of athletes and coaches all over the world. My son appreciated having these incredible role models. I would show my gratitude by fundraising to help with their out-of-country competition expenses.

Our friendship flourished. At the day's end of a successful local competition, Mitchell approached me. He reached into his sports bag and placed one of his gold medals in my hand. He told me I earned it for all my hard work. Wide-eyed, I took a deep breath and thanked him. This was a golden moment for me to treasure.

Years later, in 2004, Marc competed in the Soke Cup Chito-Ryu Karate-Do International Championship being hosted in Newcastle, Australia. There, he earned a gold medal in the men's kata division. I was proud of him and reported this to our local newspaper. A reporter contacted Marc in Japan and a write-up with a huge photo was put in the newspaper. I wished I could have been with my son at that special time in his life. For me, this article reflected the huge impact that karate had on my son's life.

When I first met Augusta, we were older than most of the karate students in our dojo. This woman was a black belt in traditional karate. I was impressed to see her in a small group that committed to giving extra time to practice the art of Kobujutsu, (weapons). Farmers during the feudal times of Japan used their farming tools as weapons to protect their family and themselves from danger. Two examples that I became aware of are, the bo, a wooden handle of a rake and the sai, fashioned from a farmer's pitchfork.

Our paths would cross more often when we discovered that her daughter, Lisa, and my son, Marc, had earned a place on the Nova Scotia Karate Team. As the saying goes, this was the beginning of a beautiful friendship.

After a class, Augusta surprised me with a dinner invitation for the following Saturday. She would take me to her favourite seaside restaurant in St. Margaret's Bay. When we finished our meal, she passed me an envelope saying, "You can open it now or later if you wish." With childlike glee, I opened it immediately.

This envelope contained a card with the picture of a toy train engine blowing puffs of smoke as it climbed a steep mountain. Its caption was, 'I think I can, I think I can'. It was overwhelming to see Augusta's handwritten note inside which read, 'I know you can'. My tears began to flow. Her thoughtfulness meant the world to me. When I could speak, I thanked her.

To end our evening, Augusta drove to the nearby sandy shore of Queensland Beach. We were close to the water's edge but could not see the ocean because a thick blanket of fog had rolled in. We enjoyed the fact that the sound of the mighty ocean could not be silenced.

As if by magic, a flock of birds flew out from the dense fog and soared above us. We watched them fly up the beach. Then as mysteriously as they had appeared, the birds returned and vanished into the fog from whence they came. She told me this was a good omen. I was and am still deeply moved by that time we spent together. Augusta's extraordinary spirit is like no other.

*****

My son and I were psyched to take part in a weekend karate clinic which would begin on a sandy beach. Breathing in the salty air and feeling my feet in the sand felt euphoric.

We would finish our first day of training with a run that took us a far distance down the beach and back. Not having the lengthy stride and fitness of the others, I lagged behind. Many of the karateka were already on their way back. As I continued to run as best I could, I began to feel discouraged seeing that everyone off in the distance had finished. Then I heard their voices; they were chanting, "Ell en ... Ell en" Several began to run towards me. Senseis Doug Chetwynd and Sensei Ralph d'Entremont were among them. When Sensei d'Entremont said, "We will run with you." I felt something explode inside of me and I lunged forward. Upon reaching the finish line, I bent over totally exhausted and feeling incredibly fulfilled.

This karate camp included the value of camaraderie. At the end of our day, we gathered around a campfire. Sensei Gary Walsh pulled out his guitar and invited all to sing along. For sure, working together and playing together cultivates a great sense of well-being.

Indoor training the next day, focused on a variety of takedowns. I was working with a guy at my belt level but much younger and taller. I could not budge him and was getting frustrated. He, on the other hand, had no problem at all taking me down. I saw that Sensei Milton Bourque was heading in our direction. He too was shorter than my partner. Sensei Bourque then performed an effortless takedown on him. This sensei emphasized the importance of good technique. He told me that with practice, I would be capable of doing this.

It was at this camp, I met Eileen Doucet, a dedicated black belt who also devoted her time to planning karate clinics. When the next one was to take place in her area, she drove five hours plus to pick me up and invited me into her home. Eileen shared the beauty of her seaside community and introduced me to its famously delicious rappie pie. I admired her positive attitude and commitment to a healthy lifestyle. A special friendship had begun.

*****

I decided to donate my cookies to a fundraiser that was taking place in our dojo training area. The money raised would help to purchase additional bogu chest and head gear for sparring. It was there, while sitting on a pile of mats and eating one of my cookies that Sensei Delaney began telling me about the Vikings.

Before they set sail, they would go to the wise one in their village for a rune reading. If the runes said that the time was not right, these fearless warriors would wait. This fascinated me.

Sensei Delaney went on to say he had his own set of twenty-five runes (twenty-four had their own symbol and one was blank). They were similar in shape and feel but each one had a very different meaning. Sensei explained that the runes are kept in a pouch and are not to be used by anyone but their owner.

He asked if I had any questions. So, I asked if he would give me a rune reading. He said that the following Tuesday at 6 pm would be the perfect time and suggested I bring some of my cookies to his home in the north end of the city. The most I had hoped for was a 'maybe' answer to my question. I told him I was not familiar with that area. Mitchell was nearby and offered to drive me. Sensei agreed so everything was a go.

When the fundraiser was over, Mitchell walked me to my car. He said that to his knowledge no students had yet been invited to Sensei Delaney's home and that included him. He then added that since he was driving me, he too should get some of my cookies. We both enjoyed a good laugh. I never thought that my cookies would have such bargaining power.

On February 8, 1994, Mitchell and I were ringing sensei's doorbell. He greeted us with a broad welcoming grin and reached out for the cookies, saying that after the rune reading, he would brew tea to go with them.

This was an evening like no other. On the kitchen table were a pouch and a rectangular wooden board with a unique design showing three defined spaces. Sensei said that he had made it and his hand never left the board from the beginning of its design to the end. He said it was a portal.

My rune reading began when he handed me a pouch and instructed me to put my left hand in it if I was right-handed. He told me to allow the runes to slip through my fingers and thumb. They felt exceptionally smooth to my touch. Sensei Delaney told me I would sense when to remove just one to place on the board.

This was my spirit rune which can only be drawn once in your life. The symbol of mine was identified as Cruz, wild ox. He said within me was great strength, vitality, and perseverance; adding that I had the gift of divination. While processing this, I returned the rune to the pouch. Once again, I felt the now familiar runes. Sensei suggested I concentrate on something I could use help with. This time I would draw three runes, one at a time. Each had its own space waiting. The first rune was identified as Berkana, birch. Sensei said that it indicated the beginning of a journey with new life experiences.

Upon drawing the second, I was once again looking at Cruz, my spirit rune, drawn earlier. Sensei Delaney said it was reaffirming I had inner strength. I was surprised that my spirit rune would appear again.

The third rune was identified as Kanu, fire, immensely powerful. Sensei told me in a quiet reassuring voice to not be afraid but to welcome the new lifepath that was being offered to me. I could not dismiss my fear of venturing into the unknown, and yet a sense of wonder rushed over me. I had concentrated on my need of courage. When I told sensei this, he said it was within me and that I just had to tap into it. This left me hopefully optimistic about my future.

Sensei then rose and tended to his kettle. He came back to the table, meticulously cleared it and put his runes away. A whistling sound signaled the water was ready. I hoped our evening would end with sipping on tea, eating a cookie or two, and listening to some of sensei's entertaining stories. I was not disappointed.

Sensei Delaney at one point, set his teacup down, stood up, and excused himself. He returned with an apology for taking so long and a vintage photograph album. The album's pages were filled with black and white and coloured photos. He then took Mitchell and me down memory lane as he leafed through the pages.

Not thinking it out, I asked if I could make copies of some photos. Sensei tilted his head in his familiar way and then agreed.

Writing this, I smile, remembering one photo was permanently affixed to the page. When sensei got up from his chair to find his scissors, I understood the look of ultimate shock on Mitchell's face. When sensei returned, I quickly apologized for asking too much of him. He said, "It's okay, it will just cost you more cookies."

He then began cutting the photo out of his treasured album. He made me promise to not give copies to anyone. I told him that I would not disappoint him. Within a few days, I returned the original photos along with an abundance of cookies.

Eight years later in Japan, I sat with Soke in a small room near the dojo training space. I showed him some personal family photos that I had brought.

The last two photos were of his dad's visit to Nova Scotia. Soke was surprised. He told me that he had never seen them before. I wanted to give them to him, however, that would mean breaking a promise. Trusting my growing intuition, I felt I was meant to be Sensei Delaney's messenger and gifted them on his behalf. Soke was pleased. He then rose from the low-lying table and carefully placed the photos on a ledge near the large, framed photo of his dad. Upon my return home, I wasted no time in telling Sensei Delaney what I had done. He immediately nodded and put my anxiousness to rest. He said he was pleased with what I had done.

*****

I want to share another intriguing encounter which took place in the latter part of the same year as my rune reading. Both addressed how my life would unfold.

While pulling weeds from my front lawn, I looked up from my tedious, strength-building exercise to find that a young woman was standing there. She introduced herself as Donna, my temporary new neighbour. Donna was friendly and interested in knowing about her new surroundings, so I invited her in for coffee.

The following week she asked me to visit a psychic with her. I declined but she continued to persist. I felt this must be important to her, so I agreed, adding I had no intention of having a reading.

On a crisp October day, we arrived at the home of her friend who had invited the psychic to be present. The taller and younger of the two women immediately approached me saying it was nice to see me again. I assured her we had never met. Her response was, "Then it was in another lifetime." She obviously was the physic. The other woman welcomed us and began to make tea. Donna and her friend shared their news since last they met while Dorothy-Lee spoke to me of the suffering and death of a dear friend. I could feel her pain. Then she stood up and said, "Come with me."

I followed her into a small bedroom and was prepared to tell her a reading was not necessary. When I heard her say she had an important message for me from God, I gave her my complete attention. His message was, 'entitlement to my life.'

With the use of cards, Dorothy-Lee went on to tell me there was much waiting for me to discover and that I was meant to have an extraordinary life. She spoke of young people coming and going, and a lot of international travel for me. It felt good to be told the time had come to concentrate on myself and not so much on others. Her words of, "Your feet can find the door, but your hand cannot find the doorknob, but it will." impacted me with a visual of exactly how I was feeling, and it gave me hope.

She continued on saying, "You will always look younger than your age and young people will be attracted to you." Dorothy-Lee prepared me, saying significant people would come into my life. She told me when it was time for them to leave, I shouldn't let it get me down. This woman accurately identified the difficulties I had experienced over the course of my life and in my marriage. She proclaimed my new life would unfold like a book, adding I would actually write a book someday and it would be published.

Dorothy-Lee confided that she encountered few people with the ability to make profound life changes; she was giddy telling me I was one of them. She described me as 'a bird in a cage and that someday I would set myself free'. She told me that I would one day have a home of my own with flowers all around it. She then said that I could achieve anything I put my mind to.

This extraordinary woman sensed that my mom had passed on. She said that even in death my mom would take care of me. Dorothy-Lee handed me an audible recording of my reading so I could revisit its wealth of information. She wanted to stay in touch, adding it was not an invitation she often extended.

I thanked her and left the room with lots to process. I would receive only two more readings then Dorothy-Lee disappeared as unexpectedly as she had appeared in my life. I marvel at the fact that I have indeed written this book, and gratefully include her within its pages.

*****

Much of my life had been about doing what I thought was expected of me. My training in karate gave me a much broader and healthier prospective. With this, the quality of my life improved significantly.

Shiko dachi, also referred to as the horse stance, taught me the rewards of endurance and willpower. I learned to get into its low stance which required perfect posture and stillness. The practice of this is to develop muscular and mental strength.

My first attempts were short-lived. When my body started to sweat and quiver, I would immediately stand up. I was told to focus on controlling my breathing and to persevere. This exercise indeed had a powerful influence on me. The more effort I put into it, the stronger I became both physically and emotionally.

It saddened me when Sensei Michael Delaney passed away in 2003. This was far too soon in his life. My son's flight from Japan arrived just in time for him to attend the funeral. Sensei had been our teacher, mentor, and hero. I will forever be grateful for his presence in my life.

Five years later, another remarkable sensei and mentor of mine, Sensei Robert Gascoigne, passed on at the age of seventy. He too had taught my son and me many valuable lessons.

I will never forget that once before formally beginning a karate class, Sensei Gascoigne informed us that a severe beating had taken place in our city over the weekend. I had never seen him distraught. "I do not want any of you to be a victim." he said vehemently.

We were lined up by belt rank. He moved about, reminding us to always be aware of our surroundings and to protect ourselves. He then came and stood by me. He said to everyone, "Look at me and look at her. Do you think she has a chance of defending herself?" He surveyed all their faces then fixed on mine saying, "You can bring me down to my knees quickly and easily." Sensei Gascoigne had everyone's attention when he told me the element of surprise and timing could save my life. Immediately following this, sensei said that if I were to firmly grab him by his groin, he would quickly drop to the floor.

He then said, "Let's get training." He walked to the front of the dojo and began our karate class with the traditional bowing. Sensei had us stretching, running, doing sit ups and more running. We then all worked on perfecting our techniques and kata. When the class was over, Sensei Gascoigne said, "Remember to never let your guard down or give up on yourself." He then added, "If any one of you need me day or night, call me and I will be there for you." Sensei Gascoigne made it possible for me to go home not feeling terrified about what happened on the weekend but empowered. I will always remember his fearless presence.

Sensei Michael Delaney and Sensei Robert Gascoigne were indeed larger than life, and their legacy lives on in all of their students. They were comrades with indomitable spirits. Each shared their courageous and comical life adventures to entertain and inspire. Their stories will continue to be retold at karate gatherings, so people who never got to meet them will hear their message of living life to the fullest.

*****

Before heading off to Calgary in 2019, I had a pleasant visit with Sensei Delaney's wife, whom he referred to over the years as "my Cheryl" From time to time, I would see sensei's two young boys, William and Gregory, as they were growing up. Now, I sat in the kitchen with these two personable young men and was telling them their dad would boast about them with immense pride.

I shared stories they had never heard which filled the room with laughter. There were also moments of silence as each of us took pause to reflect. I assured them that their dad's influence was life enriching for many. Cheryl stood up and was about to leave the kitchen. She said to me, "I have something I know Mike would want you to have." She returned with an oval stone he had painted. It was in the image of a ladybug. I will treasure this gift always.

I made great efforts to find a way to get in touch with Sensei Gascoigne's wife, Agnes. I wanted her to know the powerful impact her husband had on my son and me. It surprised her to get my telephone call. This was understandable since we had never met.

I shared some stories about her husband. One was about Santa arriving at the dojo one night at the end of class. With some 'ho, ho, hos,', he called out, "Bob, it's good to see you." Sensei Gascoigne had been distracted and turned with a curious expression on his face. As he moved closer, he asked, "Do I know you?" Santa's reply was instant, "Bob, I have known you since you were a boy and look at us now, we both wear black belts."

Agnes had not been aware of this and laughed out loud. When she was able to speak, she said, "That sounds like something Bob would do." I also shared how Sensei Gascoigne told my son and me to call him Bob when outside the dojo. She thought it hilarious with my son's immediate response of, "Hai Sensei" (Yes, Sensei). Neither my son nor I could comply because it would be like calling Superman, Clark. Agnes now was aware of how much her husband had impacted our lives.

I am not sure if I found karate or if it found me, but I am absolutely sure I began to thrive because of it. It shone a bright light on my dark days, helping me to find my true self and to explore my potential. I was inspired by my fellow karateka who motivated me and will be forever grateful to each and every one.

There are heroes in our world. It is a privilege for me to have the opportunity to pay tribute to my karate heroes.

Chapter 11:
Magical Christmas of 1999

This is a unique and wonderful story based on my chance meeting with a polite, very charming, young Frenchman. When I first saw him, he was walking through the doors of the Atlantic Karate Club. He was among several who were checking out the karate class that evening.

I was told to take the small group to the back of the dojo and acquaint them with the style of Chito-Ryu Karate Do and to teach them some basic stances. This was part of my karate training as my belt rank continued to rise.

At the end of the class, a member of the group I worked with, approached me. He was the only one who had worn a *gi*. He politely introduced himself with his engaging French accent, "I am Fabien Massol from the South of France." He thanked me for sharing this style of karate. He told me he had prior training in a different style and wished to attend more of these classes during his short stay in Canada.

I told him he was welcome and that he just had to fill out a form. Then I told him that my daughter would be taking her grade 11 in Brittany, France. I explained that the paperwork was challenging and stressful to deal with. He immediately offered to translate. I accepted and appreciated his kindness. Before leaving the dojo that night, I introduced him to my son, Marc. Next class, I invited Fabien to come to our home to meet the rest of our family. He would become Amanda's hero, easing her stress before she set off to

France. Shortly after she settled into the Bréhin household, she received a telephone call. It was Fabien asking how she was doing.

Fabien and Marc bonded. Fabien let it be known that all he had brought with him from home was his guitar, a backpack full of clothes, and his old karate *gi*. When he asked me where he could purchase a new one, I offered to deliver one to his Halifax apartment, I was more confident about driving in the city. I heard guitar music when I knocked on his door and was pleased to discover that it was Fabien.

I was invited to stay for a while. With amplifier on and guitar in hand, Fabien sang two of his favourite Jean-Jacques Goldman songs, 'Peur de rien blues' ('afraid of nothing when playing guitar), and the delightful, 'Il y a' (conjuring up nostalgic imagery such as a grandma, school, church and a cafe). I totally enjoyed my visit.

A few days later, I took Fabien to a shopping mall. A music store caught his eye and in he went. I followed behind, hearing him ask permission to play a piano. As he began to play, I saw his hands moving effortlessly over the keys. I was enthralled. The store associate, who had walked away, came back looking pleasantly surprised. We were Fabien's audience, applauding and adding a Bravo or two when he finished.

What started out as a six-month stay in Canada, turned into three incredible years. I met his kind dad José early on, when he flew in for a brief stay. Shortly after that, Fabien's older sister, Delphine, came for a visit. She was good-natured and had the same attractive brown eyes and dark hair as her brother.

She and I faced the challenge of carving out a new path in our lives. Our time together was brief, but I became well aware of her inner strength. One day, as I confided an important wish of mine to her, she held up her hand with fingers crossed saying, "I will do this for as long it takes to help make your dream come true." Before returning to Paris, Delphine invited me to visit, so she could show me the city. We were kindred spirits and kept in touch, communicating the changes in our lives. She became my dear friend reminding me to never give up.

Fabien's sweetheart, Sylvie, came to visit him. Young, attractive, and courageous; it was a joy to spend time with her. She went back to France, finished her schooling, and returned to Canada. She set a goal to learn to speak English. Fabien gladly extended his stay in Canada. He worked hard to earn his first-degree black belt rank in Chito-Ryu Karate Do while Sylvie continued to put her best efforts forth to join in the conversations around her. I was happy to see them both receive their certificates of accomplishment. Sylvie told me she felt proud of herself, and it would always be a highlight in her life.

The clock was ticking for their return to France. They would leave just before Christmas day. Since they had to vacate their apartment prior to leaving, it was my pleasure to invite them to spend their remaining days in Canada under my roof. They were going home with a plan in the making, which I assumed had to do with a wedding. I too had a plan; mine was to invite an early magical Christmas.

Preparations were taking place. Christmas carols were playing, and there was eggnog to drink. Our tree stood waiting to be decorated. Strings of lights and boxes filled with ornaments were brought out. Amanda was present but, unfortunately, Marc was not because he was attending university in Hakodate, Japan. The telephone was our back up to share our celebration.

As soon as the last ornament was placed, the strings of lights on our tree were switched on, giving the room a festive, colourful glow. Fabien and Sylvie took time to enjoy the moment and then went upstairs to take care of some last minute packing. When they returned, I pointed out two brown paper wrapped packages under the tree.

Fabien saw his name on one and Sylvie's was on the other. A short message read: Special Delivery – Open immediately. Their eyes outshone the lights on the tree. Fabien put on his Santa's helper hat while Sylvie adjusted her reindeer antlers on her head.

This was a day filled with joy as we recalled our happy times together; one was Fabien getting his Canadian Driver's license using my car. As we continued to relive our treasured memories, we enjoyed a tasty evening meal of fresh fruit, cheese, and yummy chicken pineapple casserole. When we were done, we made our way to the living room. Nightfall emphasized the glowing lights on our beautiful tree.

Then I announced, "It's time for Amanda and me to give you your Christmas Eve gifts." Over the last couple of years, Fabien had learned that our Christmas gifts could be purchased or handmade. He excused himself and went flying upstairs. He returned with several wrapped presents.

Our gift to Fabien was a Canadian 'Eh t-shirt' and for Sylvie, a nightgown. They in turn gave Amanda a CD of music they had compiled and some delicious chocolate. I was thrilled to receive a collection of Jean-Jacques Goldman's music on a disc.

A special moment began as I turned the Christmas music down to a whisper and handed Fabien a big, colourfully illustrated, hardcover book. In 1978, Marc had received this from Santa. It was T'was the Night Before Christmas. Amanda and I smiled at each other as Fabien, still wearing his red Santa Helper hat, began to read aloud.

As he read, he paused from time to time, savouring the contents of the pages. When the story came to an end, he looked boy-like as he gently closed the book. Then we all broke out singing, "We wish you a Merry Christmas."

I declared it was time to hang our stockings. Fabien and Sylvie's stockings were waiting for them under our twinkling Christmas tree. It was most heartwarming to see them being hung up. My apartment had a sunken living room, the creamy looking wrought iron railing of the upper level was a perfect spot for Santa to find them.

We had just one more important thing to do before heading off to bed. Fabien got the tray of bright orange carrots and placed it on the table for Santa's, aka Père Noël's, reindeer. I had made my peanut butter chocolate chip cookies and Sylvie carefully put them nearby. Then Amanda added to this, a tall glass of milk.

We hugged goodnight. Then Amanda and me received several kisses on each cheek. We were told that more than one kiss means you are special. I watched these young adults scurry up the stairs like little children.

Early next morning, Amanda knocked on Fabien and Sylvie's bedroom door. They opened it, rubbing their sleepy eyes. Urgently, she told them she had heard a commotion and asked them to go downstairs with her. They followed close behind.

Waiting in the living room, I watched them freeze halfway down the stairs because of what they saw. There he was, Santa. He was filling the last Christmas stocking. Discovering that he had been caught, Santa looked up and his 'ho, ho, ho's' filled the air.

The astonished couple finished coming down and were still processing. Their bewilderment only increased when Santa called them by name and talked about events in their lives. He then personally handed them their Christmas stockings. They excitedly gave Santa hugs. This was a sight to behold.

With hands on his hips and a tilt of his head, Santa confessed why he was standing in my living room before Christmas day. He explained that this year a little elf whispered in his ear. He then said there was much to do, and he had to get back to the North Pole. He gave me a wink as I slyly handed him a can of cookies to take with him. Then Santa rang his bell many times and called out to his reindeer. He wished us all a very Merry Christmas and then was gone from our sight. We could hear his jolly 'ho, ho, ho's' fade into the distance. Our special Christmas time was feeling so right!

We noticed that Santa had taken the time to devour all the cookies and milk left out for him. We noticed that his reindeer had liked the mega carrots because that plate was empty too. Then we saw the presents Santa had left for us under the tree.

Our names were clearly marked on the top of each one. We cheerfully ripped open our presents and random squeals of, 'look what I got', echoed throughout the room. Like children, we sat on the floor and took turns playing the game of Pick-up Sticks.

Mid-morning, we took a break for a tasty brunch of bacon egg muffins, cheeses, fruits, and dark chocolate. The mouth-watering smell of the turkey roasting in the oven reminded us to leave room for Christmas dinner. This would include an assortment of fresh vegetables and homemade summer savoury potato, bread stuffing. Cranberry sauce, and my homemade bright yellow cucumber relish would be in dishes nearby. For dessert, I had made frozen chocolate mocha cheesecake drizzled with a rich chocolate sauce. It would be garnished with a luscious half slice of a red strawberry with its vibrant green calyx.

The next day, Sylvie and Fabien headed for the airport. There were no tears when we parted, knowing our precious friendship would bring many more good times to share.

Chapter 12:
Rewards of Journeys
and Scary Flight

Some events can stand out in one's mind as a who would have thought this could have happened to me. In my case, August, September, and October 1997 were perfect examples.

When my daughter's flight was nearing to take her to France for a school year, she told me she was feeling a bit scared. Amanda confessed that she wished she were flying towards rather than away from me. I wanted to spare her this anxiety and came up with a plan.

Both of us needed the luck of the Irish on our side. I had met a fun-loving young woman named Aedín, when she was visiting her parents for a few months. Her dad was on a contract. Upon its completion, he and Aedín's mum would return home to Ireland. Learning where she was from, I excitedly told her of the love I had for my Irish and Scottish roots.

With her delightful Irish accent, she extended an open invitation for me to visit her someday, promising to show me the gaiety of Dublin and some of her other favourite places. We kept in touch, and during one of our conversations, Aedín told me she was temporarily living in Guildford, England.

The timing was perfect. It would be great to get together again with my dear friend and hopefully travel to nearby Ireland. My stay in the land of her Majesty the Queen, provided me the opportunity to cross the English Channel to France and help my daughter settle in. I made the call to merry old England. Aedín was excited to hear from me and before our conversation was over, she not only looked forward to my visit, but told me that a short Ryanair flight would take us to Dublin.

I gave my daughter the good news that I would be leaving Canada before her, and we would meet up in St. Malo. It all felt surreal, and my head was spinning. Amanda was relieved and, as she hugged me, she whispered, "My wish is really coming true." Her hug energized me to get busy deciding on what surprises I would take. My list would start with her favourite cookies.

Our local international airport was small and offered a two-hour plus flight to Toronto where I could board a connector flight to London. When I arrived, I found the massive and crowded Heathrow Airport very unnerving. It was buzzing with countless travellers. Some of them kindly pointed me in the right direction.

Once I got to arrivals, my immediate attention was drawn to a cabby holding a sign above his head that had my name on it. This jolly chap would take me to Guildford. Along the way, he asked where I was from and if I had heard of Eric Clapton. He brought my attention to the Queen Victoria Pub telling me that Phil Collins had many a pint there. Within days, I too would end up having a pint with my friend in that stately pub and we would also stroll by Phil Collin's home.

While the kind cabbie was retrieving my luggage from the boot of his car, I gazed at the row of rustic bricked townhouses. Aedín stepped out from one of them with open arms. I loved her wit and great sense of humour. Her smile, striking blue eyes, and lilting accent were a breath of fresh air for me.

I was enchanted by our outings. We meandered alongside a picturesque narrow canal in Guildford which was busy with the comings and goings of small boats. Several arched bridges crossed over this waterway, inviting pedestrians to be able to explore the neighbourhoods and shops on either side. I felt intoxicated with the smell of the rich green grass and the sight of gorgeous weeping willows that were the largest and lushest I had ever seen. On another outing, I basked in the welcoming atmosphere of woodsy Surrey and the unforgettable view of its stone church with its Anglo-Saxon tower.

The clustered houses and the feel of cobblestones beneath my feet put a spring in my step. Another fond memory made with my friend was a tasty meal and a pint at a George Gale & Company Ltd. Pub that dated back to 1847.

I learned several unfamiliar terms. I liked the sound of, 'that's brilliant,' identifying something amazing. The word knackered had to be explained to me and it had nothing to do with being under the influence; it was about being tired. We had a good laugh over that one. At another time, before we headed out the door for a walk, Aedín suggested I wear a jumper. I told her I had not brought one. She then handed me one of her sweaters. My brain had been thinking of a certain kind of dress. It was so amusing.

I traveled on the underground subway and climbed up a steep narrow stairway to the light of day. There, I was greeted with a panoramic view of the magnificent Wembley Stadium.

Being in London made my heart skip a beat. As a child, I had sung, London Bridge is falling down, and holding hands with my playmates, we moved around in a circle, singing, ring around the roses, a pocket full of posies, ashes, ashes, we all fall down. I had no idea the lyrics referenced horrific events like the bubonic plague of 1665. As my attention shifted from that dark past to the present, a now vibrant city stretched out before me. Here I was, a witness to better times.

During my visit, I gazed upon the famous gold-faced Big Ben clock tower at the House of Parliament, Westminster Abbey, and the helmeted London Bobbies in their crisp uniforms. For fun, I stepped inside one of London's iconic red telephone booths to see how it felt looking out. The red double-decker buses made me feel like I was in a scene from a movie.

I watched the street performers while enjoying chips for lunch at Covent Garden. I was drawn to a formally dressed concert-like trio and was spellbound by their performance. The black and white images of England that I had watched on a projector screen as a child, was alive and in colour right before my eyes.

The day came when Aedín and I excitedly boarded our Ryanair flight. While flying low over England, I saw the quaint villages and a magnificent estate with pastureland and forest. Seeing people riding on horseback brought to mind Robin Hood and his band of merry men living in

Sherwood Forest. Those stories of robbing from the rich to give to the poor had fired my imagination when I was a child.

We were on our way to Ireland, the country of Aedín's birth. When we arrived in Dublin and my feet touched its soil, I sensed a tingle like no other. It felt as if I had once lived there. Her relatives and friends made me feel over the moon. I strolled the charming streets and visited the shops. The atmosphere in the local pubs was one of gaiety and laughter as its patrons enjoyed the company of one another. During a future visit to Ireland, I was enchanted by Galway, and took pleasure in my time with her parents, Sal and Colm whose home was in coastal Connaught. Breathtaking sights and hilarious moments of joy and laughter abounded; but that's another story.

When the time came for us to fly back to England, I felt scared knowing I would be on my own to navigate the meeting up with my daughter. However, I would do whatever it took for her. This would involve taking a train and a bus to Portsmouth and then boarding a ferry for a nine-hour nighttime crossing of the Channel to St. Malo in France.

My journey started out well. After being dropped off near the train station, I decided to pick up a snack for the long day ahead; it would be root beer and a bag of potato chips. I looked for my train and could see there were two waiting. I chose the one that appeared to be pointing in the right direction, descended the steep stairs, and boarded.

Once seated, I told a passenger I was going to Portsmouth. He immediately told me I was on the wrong train. I hurried up the stairs, then crossed the platform, and ran down more stairs to the other train. I was out of breath but filled with relief. When the train pulled away, I got out my snack.

Opening the pop, I heard a loud fizzing sound, then I watched as its contents jetted into the air landing, on the passengers around me. They were quiet, even sombre, when I first sat down. Now, chaos. They came to life, twisting around, leaping out of their seats, frantically dabbing at the spots of dark, sweet liquid.

No one spoke, as I babbled on with my apologies. I felt terrible that I had caused such a commotion. Then an older lady gave me tissues to wipe my face and jacket. Sometime later, while sitting on an outdoor bench waiting for the bus to the ferry, I ate my potato chips and drank the remains of my pop.

When I arrived at the seaport, I relaxed and engaged in a chat with a friendly young man. He walked me to my gate. Once aboard the huge multi-level ferry, I found my way to a seating area where an elderly woman sat nearby. She moved closer to tell me that she was a widow and despite the sad recent loss of her husband, she refused to give up on life.

This sweet woman then invited me to join her for something to eat, but I had to decline because I was too exhausted. She returned with a sandwich and tea for me. I thanked her and offered her money which she quickly refused. I told her she was an Earth Angel just before drifting off to get some much-needed sleep. When I awoke, she was gone. The ferry was almost completely docked when I saw my daughter and Yann waving excitedly. I melted into their welcoming hugs.

It was an hour to Rennes, Brittany's capital. I soaked up the views of the coastal fortified city of St. Malo, bordered by golden sandy beaches. It felt like I was back in time, on the page of some history book. The Bréhin family invited me into their cream-coloured stucco home with its triangular roof, covered in locally sourced dark gray slate tiles. It felt great to be sitting in the glassed sunroom, off their dining room, with its beautiful view of their treed backyard. I enjoyed a tasty meal with the family that Chantal had prepared to make me feel welcome.

Amanda took me upstairs to her bedroom. She sat on the bed while I opened my suitcase and pulled out a plush stuffed rabbit, olbas, and tea tree oils, and peanut butter chocolate chip cookies. She gobbled down several immediately. We decided it would be okay if she wanted to keep them to herself. After all, they were her comfort food, a reminder of home.

We had the best time together. When she told me she felt her stay would be a good one, my heart felt at ease. I knew my daughter was in the best of hands. Yann drove us back to St. Malo where we hugged farewell. I boarded the ferry, made my way to the upper deck and watched my daughter and Yann fade into the distance. I could no longer hold back my tears. It was going to be rough having Amanda so far away for such a long time.

I found the daytime crossing soothing. The blue sky meshed in with the calm blue sea. I went inside the vessel and heard music playing. It was Louie Armstrong singing, What a Wonderful World. In that moment, I felt the truth of those lyrics. I had an amazing getaway, and my daughter was where she was meant to be. It really was a wonderful world. I returned to the outdoor deck and glimpsed what I thought to be the brilliant white cliffs of Dover that I had heard so much about.

When we reached land, I was on my own again to make my way. This time, I hoped for less drama. I found the ticket agent in Portsmouth very entertaining, perched high and enclosed in glass with his microphone. I was determined to not get lost, so I clearly stated my train ticket was for Guildford, England. To the delight of those nearby, his voice rang out, "You are *in* England." Amidst the collective laughter, I placed my money in the tray that disappeared and reappeared with my change and ticket. I felt like applauding his performance and bowing to our audience, but I had a bus and a train to catch.

I arrived and boarded a red double-decker bus that would take me to Aedín's place. On my last night, we raised our glasses of Jameson whisky saying, 'Sláinte'. We all remained in good health to enjoy more good times together.

I would fly from Gatwick Airport, which was much smaller than Heathrow, to make my way home. Just when I felt I had escaped drama-free, a loud siren screamed. Vendor doors quickly began sliding and closed. An airport employee told me that shutdown mode was in progress. Apprehension began to set in, but thankfully this didn't last long, and I was glad to have been checked in for my flight. The security guard suggested I hurry to my gate, so off I ran. Eventually, I arrived safely back home.

Amanda and I both learned that if you give into scary feelings and forfeit your journey, you can cheat yourself of the many joys that are waiting to be had.

*****

October 6, 1997, brought an unexpected adventure. I had been back home for only ten days and welcomed my brother Stan's invitation to join him and two other guys on a flight over our city of Halifax. It would be a first for me in a small aircraft and I looked forward to it.

His brother-in-law, Dave, would pilot the four-seater plane. I felt fortunate to be the one taking the seat of the guy who couldn't make it and would sit back and enjoy the ride.

Being inside a hangar of the Halifax International Airport was amazing. This felt very different from commercial airline travel. Dave walked around the small aircraft as he did his pre-flight inspection. He told us its frame was fabric covered and sprayed with a special coating.

The guys and I pushed this light weighted plane outside. We boarded and taxied to the runway to await take-off confirmation. Once we had the go-ahead, the pilot revved the engine and we sped down the runway. Lift off was exhilarating.

At first, the continuous loud sound of the single engine was hard on my ears. The pilot and my brother in the co-pilot position wore headphones, which no doubt dampened the sound for them. I began to acclimatize, and soon I was lost in the spectacular aerial view. It was a gorgeous autumn day. There was a clear blue sky above, and below a scattering of vibrant red, orange, yellow and brown foliage amid a forest of spruce and fir trees.

Soon we were flying over the two bridges that connect the cities of Halifax and Dartmouth. We circled over Citadel Hill. This was my first bird's-eye view of its star-shaped design and my city of Halifax. It was an absolute thrill for me.

Dave turned in his pilot's seat and raised his voice over the din to ask me if there was anywhere else that I wanted to go. It felt like I had won a lottery. I asked him to fly us under the bridges and got a quick 'no can do.' Then, on a more serious note, I asked if he would fly over Peggy's Cove.

This cove is 43 km southwest of Halifax by car. I never dreamed I would have the opportunity to fly over it and was elated when Dave gave the thumbs-up. Our route would take us over the subdivisions where my brother and I lived next to azure lakes, winding railway tracks, quaint churches, and neighbourhood schools.

I had a huge smile on my face when I spotted our famous lighthouse. It is recognized around the world with its white exterior and red cupola, towering above the surrounding bed of rocks.

Our Atlantic Ocean at times can be fierce, producing giant, dangerous waves that crash violently against the shore. However, on this day, it was calm as the sun's light danced on its surface. We looked down at the local restaurant where lobster dinners were enjoyed by locals and visitors alike. The nearby gift shops, small church, and colourful boat sheds, complete with buoys and fish nets, were also a welcomed sight.

The surrounding area bears the scars wrought by the glaciers and the ocean tides over countless eons. This desolate rugged landscape seemed vast to me at ground level, but from above it looked like a small patch of ground, scattered with boulders of all shapes and sizes.

Seeing nearby Cranberry Cove to the northwest made my heart skip a beat. My children and I had grown to love this place. Kerry Adams, a fellow karateka and avid scuba diver, told me of it. He said that it was a unique place that offered seclusion, beauty and peacefulness.

Marc, Amanda, and I wasted no time in checking it out. We carefully followed Kerry's excellent directions and pulled over on the side of the road that offered the narrow path he had described. Excitedly, we made our way through the overgrown terrain and there it was. This small cove was charming and provided a distant view of the Peggy's Cove village and lighthouse.

On that day, Cranberry Cove shared the scent of its multicoloured wildflowers. We embraced its unique terrain which included being able to walk in a narrow, shallow waterway that emptied into the ocean. Pools of water among the rocks, held magnificent reflections for us to photograph. This hidden gem became our paradise.

I came out of my reverie and found myself back in the small flying machine. I felt the ease of an eagle as we circled, then descended for a closer look. When I heard Dave radio the airport to let them know we were heading back, I felt grateful to have had this unexpected and sublime excursion. With eyes closed, I sent my deep appreciation out into the universe.

Just minutes later, a dead silence enveloped the plane. The once annoying loud sound of its single engine literally vanished into thin air. An electric current began to race throughout my entire body leaving me dumbfounded. The pilot was focused and busy with the control panel. I remember hearing my brother ask if there was anything he could do. Dave then announced he could not restart the engine.

I listened to him calmly report our situation to the air traffic control center. He provided them with our location and altitude. Numbly, I tried to process that this was potentially life-threatening. Meanwhile, without power, this plane was descending. I heard our competent pilot answering questions. The conversation ended with Dave being told to re-establish contact after he set the aircraft down.

Amazingly, my feelings of shock, disbelief, and concern began to dissipate as I became fascinated with what was outside the windows. Not thinking, I removed my seat belt to get a better look. Dave immediately told me to put it back on, and so I did.

Rob, sitting to my left, looked scared. He leaned forward, gripped both sides of the pilot's seat from behind and put his head down. He urged me to do the same. I complied and got into this crash position.

However, something powerful within once again got me to re-engage with the outside. I turned to Rob and told him I could not do this. Again, I stretched to see the changing view. A vivid image of mine that remains is seeing a narrow, winding road with power lines amid a densely forested area.

The silence onboard was eerie. Then Dave announced that Highway 102 was in sight. It was a Saturday, and the highway was moderately busy with traffic. He gave us a heads up that those drivers on the highway would not hear us approaching.

When the wheels of the plane met the pavement, it moved forward along the 102. I felt relief and was energized.

Dave had skillfully set the plane down in an open space in the flow of the traffic. He chose the left-hand lane explaining that if we were to be hit from behind, we would go into the earth and grass that separates the twin double lane highway.

The possibility of traffic on my side of the plane was of concern. There were no side mirrors, our windows did not open for a better view, and we did not have the indicator lights of a car. After a reasonable pause, Dave maneuvered the plane over into the right-hand lane. He then removed it from the highway where a weigh station was located.

He told us to get out immediately when the plane was at a full stop. He then moved the left wing as much as possible out of harm's way. I saw nearby traffic was at a stand still, with headlights on. The other side of the highway revealed vehicles pulled over allowing spectators to watch the goings-on.

Police, fire trucks, and other emergency vehicles began arriving on the scene with sirens blaring and lights flashing. An officer from nearby Truro told me he had rushed to our location. When the news media arrived, they chose to interview me. I told the reporter this had turned into an exhilarating experience for me. I was not shaken or burdened with a fear of flying.

Prior to leaving the site, three of us who had been onboard, watched as the blue four-seater plane taxied onto the highway to take flight once again. Its owner had arrived, and the plane's malfunction had been attended to. He would pilot his plane back to the Halifax International Airport with Dave sitting alongside.

My husband was the only one at home to greet me. He came up the stairs saying he saw me on the news. He added, "This is just something else to put on your list." He then turned and headed back downstairs. I had grown used to his indifference.

The day that I walked away from a danger I had never known, would indeed go on my list of life-changing events, along with another. It was the wake-up call for me to make an important decision. I realized I had kept my head down in the crash position when it came to my marriage.

I called my daughter in France. She was shocked and upset, thinking of all the scary 'what if's'. There was no way to contact my son; he would return home on Sunday from a New Brunswick karate competition. When I told him what happened, he was shocked and gave me a big hug. I assured my children there was no need to worry about me.

An image of the plane's take off appeared in the Sunday Daily News publication, along with the eventful story. Another similar image was placed on five t-shirts with a caption of, Life Is A Highway And We're Gonna Fly It. The fifth shirt was given to the owner of the Stinson aircraft who had lent it for a fun filled flight.

The drama of our Saturday emergency landing aired that evening, and again on Monday's Live at 5 news broadcasts. Video footage included an airport mechanic assessing the failure of the aircraft's engine. He said that carburetor ice had been the problem which was the result of a temperature drop. He then praised the pilot, saying his decision-making had saved lives. Knowing four lives were spared, and that I was one of them, filled me with immense gratitude. In the future, I would refer to this news show as, Alive at 5.

Chapter 13:
The Perfect Professional Centre

Looking for the perfect way to fix a relationship or to help someone become the best version of themselves always starts with good intentions. I had spent years trying to figure out how to help solve my husband's problems which were actually beyond my control. Sadly, I got lost in the shuffle and would require lots of help to reclaim my life.

My son and daughter gave me a unique gift when I needed it most. All the emotional stresses I was carrying had begun to take a toll on me physically. Early one evening, my son knocked on my bedroom door and asked if I was alright. I replied that I just needed some rest. The truth was, I was weary and nearing hopelessness.

I could hear the muffled voices of my son and daughter in the living room, where we often gathered to discuss their hopes and dreams. I was unable to get out of my bed to join them. Marc returned to my closed door saying, "Mom, please come out and share some time with us." The sound of his voice worried me, so I pulled myself up and walked to the living room. I had expected to find them there, but instead they were in the kitchen.

There on the floor, I saw them sitting on the baby blanket we had shared many times throughout their childhood years. It brought comfort when popsicles were eaten to bring down fevers, where countless books were read, and songs sung. Also, it served as our picnic blanket where mommy's cookies were devoured. Now, it held three small wine glasses, crackers, cheese, and the bottle of wine my daughter had brought back from France. Her intentions were to keep it for the right occasion, and, apparently, this was it. Amanda patted the spot where they wanted me to sit.

Marc opened and poured the wine. He and Amanda talked about their childhood and early teenage years and thanked me for all I had done for them. I listened intently to what they each knew I needed to hear. My increasingly melancholy moods had not gone unnoticed, and this worried them. When we were out together, they could see me enjoying myself, but at home I was far from happy.

They said they would support me to start a new life. I knew our picnic had come to an end when one said, "Now you can go to your room and think about what you should do." These were the exact words I had delivered to them in times of difficulty. It was meant to empower them to think about making good choices. We hugged good night and I went to bed knowing it was the time for me to act.

I would make an important phone call to invite Lisa over for tea and cookies. In my kitchen, across from me, sat this dynamic young woman. It was hard to believe how quickly the years had flown by. I had great memories of her and my son as members of the Nova Scotia Karate Team. I admired her dedication to karate, always working on perfecting her skills. This attitude was reflective of the competent lawyer she had become.

We took time to catch up on family and friends. It felt like my mom was whispering in my ear, "Ask her" While Lisa was sipping her tea, I asked if she remembered contributing a session of legal advice at a team fundraising auction. I quickly followed up with that I had bid on and won it, and now I needed to use it. Putting her cup down she said, "Sure, Ellen. Is it regarding a will, sale of property or power of attorney?"

When I didn't respond, she stopped. Lisa then got up from her chair and came over to mine. She bent down and gave me a comforting hug. The hug was from my caring friend, while her voice was that of a competent lawyer saying, "I will take care of you." Lisa was true to her word. Without delay she counselled me and drafted a legal and binding separation agreement. Finally, I would escape from the debilitating stress I had been living with for many years.

*****

Several years would pass before I needed Lisa's help again. She gave me the address of a professional centre where she had relocated her office. A meeting was set for the following Sunday.

Lisa greeted me at its entrance with a hug. My first impression of the centre was a positive one. It housed a variety of skilled professionals. The waiting area offered comfy, dark blue leather armchairs with mahogany tables. There was a monitor above a fireplace, and a bookcase on either side. Behind the reception desk, two boardroom doors were open, revealing a magnificent view of the Bedford Basin.

She took me to the luxurious boardroom to discuss the threat I had been given of losing my alimony payments. She assured me there was no need to worry and excused herself to get some papers. I sat alone, staring out at the serene ocean basin and blue sky. I reflected back to when I was afraid to leave my marriage.

I recalled my brother Stan's reaction when I told him I was leaving my marriage. He said, "Welcome back" Noting my confusion, he went onto clarify that the 'me' he had known had been gone for a long time. He supported my decision and offered his help without any judgment or lectures. With his quick wit, he told me he would never let me go hungry, adding, "After all, you don't eat a whole lot." With this, we broke out laughing.

Lisa returned and sat across from me. With one of my freshly baked, half-eaten cookies in hand, she raised her head from her paperwork and said, "You know what? I can see you working here, sitting at the front desk greeting people and making them feel comfortable." I was flattered that she would consider me for such a position. At the end of our meeting, she gave me a hug and the telephone number of one of the owners of that professional centre. I was, in fact, in need of a job to supplement my meager income. A few days later, I contacted Marie to explore the possibility of job shadowing at the front desk of her company; I hoped it would lead to an opportunity ahead.

In the midst of chaos and trepidation, it was almost impossible for me to imagine something so wonderful was waiting just around the corner. I would indeed come to sit at that reception desk when needed. A small plaque that sat on it read, Director of First Impressions. It caught the attention of many because it was both amusing and powerful.

Everyone who came through those doors was unique and had specific needs. I gave to each my absolute best, just like the professionals they had come to see. Along with my offers of coffee, tea, or water, I assured them they were in the best hands and would be well taken care of.

Throughout the day, I watched a busy flow of professionals enter and exit the small kitchenette in clear view of my desk. I got a kick out of their facial expressions as they came out with a beverage in one hand, and a cookie or two of mine in the other.

I jokingly boasted that my cookies were full of protein for energy, and that the chocolate chips delivered a great sense of well-being. It was entertaining and hilarious to hear childlike comments of, "Yum, best cookies ever." Will you bring in more?" Along with a kind thank you, some would add that they had needed a little pick-me-up, and off they would go with an added pep in their step.

This professional centre had been carefully put together by its two keen owners, Marie and Ivan. They were diligent in their efforts to nurture an environment of harmony at the centre, which they populated with skillful professionals who provided quality services to their clients.

Marie, and her husband Dale, both genuinely kind human beings, took me under their wings. It was their daughter Ashley, who trained me in the responsibilities of the receptionist, and also who gave me an abundance of hugs when I needed them.

On my lunch breaks, a young woman named Maria filled in for me. When time permitted, we got to know more about each other. I admired her passion for the environment and the care of animals. A friendship blossomed as we began to enjoy some spare time on weekend outings.

The balcony off the boardroom offered relaxing vistas of the beautiful historic Bedford Basin. On good weather days, I would eat my lunch at one of the patio tables and watch the sailboats making their way across the water. Also, it gave me a great view of the busy A. Murray MacKay bridge.

I watched a seagull swoop by. It then climbed and soared above. I appreciated that people also could soar to great heights when given care and support.

I witnessed this while working at what I believe to be the perfect professional centre.

Chapter 14:
Disappointment Made Way For Joy

I had heard that change is a major stressor for human beings. For me, stress manifested from the fear of the unknown and a fear of disappointment. Added to these two, would be making a marital change. I would take a leap of faith that would alter the course of my life.

*****

At the tender age of twenty, I married my first boyfriend after one year of dating. I had many hopes and dreams when I came into the marriage. The years that followed brought some nice highs, but these were out numbered by far too many devastating lows. I had given my heart and soul to the relationship, but after twenty-seven years, I had to accept that no matter how much I gave of myself, it would never be enough to make our marriage a happy one.

The enormous stress and disappointment of leaving behind my familiar home and the life I had committed to for so long weighed heavily on me. It was my son and daughter who provided me with the momentum to make decisions.

I had always processed things slowly before acting. My fiery daughter, on the other hand, was born with a go for it attitude. On a day when her high school declared a storm day closure, Amanda took this opportunity to rummage through the newspaper ads. She spied some affordable apartment rentals, circled them and said, "This unexpected holiday can be the perfect day to start looking for a place to live."

The first number I called was an apartment building ten minutes away by car. It did sound interesting. Amanda said, "Mom, call back and ask if we can see it now." My immediate response was to remind her of the impending storm to which she replied, "The snow hasn't started yet, so we can get there and back before it does." I made the call, and we were on our way.

Our wait time in the lobby was brief. The superintendent arrived, introduced herself, and said the apartments in this building had two levels. She then unlocked the door that led us up a flight of stairs to the first-floor apartments and a shared laundry room. We continued up two more flights of stairs to the second-floor apartments.

The one we had come to see was at the far end of the hall, on the left. She told us that the building had been constructed in 1978; my kneejerk response was that my son was born the same year.

Once we were inside, Joan apologized for the unpleasant smell and debris, explaining that several students occupied it and seemed more focused on their studies than housekeeping. The walk-through was a blur for me, but my daughter was attentive to every detail, assessing the pros and cons. Joan ended the tour with, "So do you want this apartment?"

I replied it was very important to find a place for me and my two teenage children to live. She then informed me I would need a character reference letter, a half a month's rent deposit and the first month's rent. My face began to flush. Overwhelmed, I told her that I needed some time to think. She put her hand on my shoulder, saying, "Dear, I feel this is the perfect apartment for you and your children. I'm not supposed to, but I will give you two days to get back to me."

Amanda and I thanked this caring woman and headed home as a light snow began to fall. My daughter told me that she liked the apartment, especially its perfect location.

When we arrived home, my son had returned from an early morning university class. Amanda excitedly gave him the news. Marc wanted to see the apartment right away and offered to drive. He assured me the road conditions would still be good. Joan was as surprised as I to meet again so soon.

This time, I returned with different eyes as we stepped inside the apartment. I looked passed the cream-coloured painted wrought iron railing at a spacious open concept layout. The living room area below had a huge window that looked out onto some trees and the parking lot of another apartment building across the way. To the right were sundeck doors off a space that appeared to be a small dining room. We went down a few steps and walked through a doorway into a small galley kitchen; off to its right was a door opening to a storage and pantry area. To the left, we were able to access the dining room area. Marc was impressed to see a wraparound deck. When we stepped out, he said it would replace our backyard and we could barbeque.

Returning inside, I imagined a computer sitting on a desk in the corner close by, instead of dining room furniture. The side window nearby would let in sunlight and fresh air and would be convenient for passing barbeque utensils to the outside. Amanda suggested a small dining room table and chairs would work great in the living room space near the stairs. Before climbing to the upper level, Marc opened the door under the stairwell revealing the place for jackets and footwear; he said, "We can also store some of our stuff here."

The stairs to the upper level brought us to a large and small bedroom with closets. A linen closet, and a bathroom were also on this level. Marc and Amanda were excited and voiced how spacious the apartment was. She then drew her brother's attention to a small space that was a few steps up; it appeared to be a little loft. Joan reminded us that it was intended for a fire escape exit. Amanda suggested it could also be a neat area to read a book or to put a sleeping bag when friends slept over.

My son and daughter told me we could make this our new home. It was indeed perfect for us. The rent was unbelievably low for what we were getting, and, with my frugal ways, it was affordable. I then told Joan we would take it. I noticed she had been very attentive to my son and daughter's excitement.

Joan took me aside, and said, "I'm happy for you and your family. I'll have it cleaned and repainted after the tenants vacate next month." She then added, "You don't have to provide a character reference." I was touched by her sentiment when she gave me a hug. I would come to know that Joan had a sweet tooth. I would give her lots of my baked goods, starting with my cookies of gratitude.

The chatter as we drove back to our split entry house warmed my heart. We were leaving a much larger home but would find ways to maximize the space now awaiting us. Our attic and basement were full of baby clothes, favourite childhood toys, gym equipment, sports items, and more to sort through. We decided their dad could keep all the household furniture except for Marc's and Amanda's beds. Our apartment storage under the stairwell for sure would be jammed with items that we were not ready to let go of.

With much hard work and the help of our family and friends, we moved into Apartment 215. It was important for me that my son and daughter have their own bedrooms where they could sleep on their familiar wooden futons. I purchased a sofa bed for the living room and would sleep there. I concentrated on creating a homey atmosphere. My search began for a shelving unit with more charm than a regular bookcase. It would be the custodian of our family photos and mementos, old and new.

I narrowed my choice down to two. My absolute favourite one happened to be the more expensive, so I waited patiently for a sale. Unfortunately, it was my least favourite that went on sale. The price was phenomenal, so I decided to make it work. There were only two of them left; I chose the boxed over the display model because it fit easily into my hatchback vehicle.

Amanda and I planned to assemble it that evening. When we opened the box, it was utter disappointment to see pieces badly broken. I called the store immediately and explained my situation. The customer service agent advised me to return the item for a full refund. I told her I would rather exchange it for the display model. She said a sold sign would be put on it. I knew help would be needed to get it to my apartment so early the next morning I arrived at the store to make arrangements. Before doing so, I decided to take another look at the shelving unit. However, it was no where to be seen. Thinking Customer Service had it stowed, I went there and was met with a lot of unexpected confusion. Then the bomb was dropped; the unit was nowhere to be found. Other store locations were called on my behalf and that's when the second bomb was dropped; all were sold out. I was very upset and needed some peace of mind as to how this could have happened, so I asked to see the store manager. I wanted him to know what had taken place. The sympathetic customer service representative told me the manager was busy at the back of the store, having a morning meeting with the associates.

I made my way there, where a large group of people were gathered, and asked an associate nearby to point out the manager. He said that when the staff dispersed, I would see him sitting on top of a pile of rugs.

When the meeting ended, I hurried over. As the manager slowly stood up, he transformed into a giant right before my eyes. I describe myself as being vertically challenged, so you can imagine that we must have seemed like quite the pair.

Looking up at him, I introduced myself and shared my sad story. He, in turn, bent down to listen more closely. His story was much briefer than mine, as he said, that unfortunately, the sold sign was not placed on the shelving unit quick enough. I apologized for being overemotional and told him I would try to get over it.

He continued to surprise me with his soft voice and meek manner. He apologized profusely and then added that he could absolutely understand my disappointment. It hit home to hear him say, "The floor model was yours and now somebody else has it." It was as though he could read my mind. He said he too, felt badly. This was what I needed to hear. I was ready to leave.

As I was turning away, I was astonished to hear him say, "Wait a minute, would a $50 gift card make you happy?" I showered him with thankyous. He sent me back to Customer Service where the gift card was placed in my hand.

While walking back to the busy hardware store parking lot to my vehicle, I realized that I did not know the manager's name. I smiled as I thought to myself that his name must be André the Giant. I went home with a heart full of gratitude. To thank the manager for his understanding and generosity, the next day I returned with some cookies.

At Customer Service, I made it a point to look at the young lady's name tag. Then I said, "Joy, will you please page the manager? I have a delivery to make." She gazed at the decorative package of cookies that I was holding. The associate who had identified the manager for me just happened to be nearby. He overheard my request and quickly told Joy there was no need to page the manager because he would get him for me. I thanked him and added that I didn't mind waiting. He said, "If I bring him here, he will have to share some of those cookies with me." We all chuckled and off he went.

He soon returned with the giant, who was surprised to see me and my cookies. Before I handed them over, he confirmed that his world was peanut butter and chocolate friendly. He took me totally off guard when he bent down extremely low and asked if he could give me a hug. I happily agreed saying, "You're my hero, of course, you can." In the embrace, I felt like a hobbit.

My happy ending came after I returned the damaged unit and made my way to the shelving unit that had been my favorite all along. It was like it had been waiting there for me to take it home. This time there would be no disappointment. I had the contents of the box carefully inspected before I asked for it to be brought to the front of the store and taken to my car. I handed over the $50 gift card along with my payment.

On my way out, I spotted the manager and told him what I had done. "No one else will be getting this one but me." I declared. We both laughed and I thanked him again. As I walked away, he called out, "Your cookies are the best." I turned and called back, "You're the best."

The attractive shelving unit stood tall in my living room. It came with a wonderful memory and would be the keeper of many cherished treasures.

*****

With the year coming to an end, I stood alone looking out the window of my new home, feeling stronger than I could ever have imagined. On the eve of the year 2000, I reflected that in a span of ten months, my children and I had welcomed our family and friends into our new place, had celebrated a number of special occasions. And even got to enjoy a magical Christmas with dear newfound friends.

Important to me was that my son, who had gone off to study at a university in Japan, had his bedroom waiting for his return.

In the dark of night, outside the window I could see the pulsing lights of the city; this made me feel energized and that there was a lot out there for me to discover. Within moments, the sky filled with thunderous multicoloured fireworks.

My son called me from Japan and my daughter called from a party she was attending. With joy in our hearts, we wished each other a Happy New Year!

As I began to drift off to sleep that night, I embraced that my leap of faith, and my good choices, had brought me to a better place in life. This was positive proof that disappointment can make way for joy.

Chapter 15:
The Battlefield of Aging

I remember that unforgettable moment when I took a second glance in the mirror and said out loud to my aging reflection, "Who are you?" It reminded me of being in the home of my younger brother, Eldred, who was waiting for a memo concerning events that were coming his way. I considered this my memo from Mother Nature. It was time for me to evaluate what I saw and how it made me feel.

Aging can wreak havoc on our appearance, energy and overall attitude.

My mom didn't indulge in many beauty products to enhance her appearance. She had a jar of Pond's face cream and a daily ritual of gently applying it to her face and neck. On special occasions, she would put on lipstick and a hint of face powder.

In her younger days, my mom was a natural green-eyed beauty with a nice figure and perfect gleaming white teeth. Her smile was the one people pay lots of money to have. I saw many photos of her with her beautiful shoulder-length hair. As she got older, she decided to keep her hair short for practical reasons. I saw that her beautiful smile never got old.

One day my thoughtful sister Celie surprised our mother with a box of hair colour. She would apply it if mom wanted to hide her grey. We all agreed the color choice was a perfect match. Disappointingly, mom told Celie it had to be put on hold for when she would have time for it. Mom kept herself busy attending to the needs of others rather than her own.

I recall complimenting a woman one day, telling her she was lucky to have such nice hair. She responded that luck had nothing to do with it. She told me good hair products and choosing colours that make you feel good is what it's all about.

I experimented with my hair length, colour, and curl. I was influenced by my grown children and the ages of my much younger friends; I wanted to hold onto a youthful look and feel. I appreciated that training in karate throughout the years had kept my body fit.

Another incentive to become proactive was my stature. Many have an aerial view of the top of my head which would enable them to see my unwanted grey hair.

I discovered a new hair design centre within walking distance of where I lived. Professional hair stylists guided students in training while they practiced on clients. This scenario sounded inviting and more affordable for me. As soon as I entered the establishment, I felt the presence of positive energy and heard the buzz of hair dryers blowing, scissors snipping and, the chatter of professional stylists in the making. I was greeted by an engaging well-groomed woman standing behind a counter. She introduced herself as Jeanette and asked what she could do for me.

I asked about customer satisfaction and price. She then put my mind at ease with both answers. Just as I was about to make an appointment, she said, "If you like, I can see if someone is available now." This was totally unexpected. I accepted gleefully and said I was in desperate need of a cut and colour. She then excused herself and returned with the name of the student assigned to me and her level of experience. I would meet her along with her supervisor in approximately 10 minutes.

Jeanette then asked, "Would you care for a coffee or perhaps some water while you wait?" It was early morning and a black coffee sounded great. I waited on a nearby bench, sipping my coffee and marvelling at how quickly everything was unfolding.

I surveyed the salon's layout and surrendered to all that it had in store for me. I liked the open concept that revealed rows of workstations. Male and female students were pleasantly engaged with their clients, as their hands busily applied their ongoing acquired skills. It was a diverse, multicultural group. Some looked like they were fresh out of high school, while others were closer to thirty or forty. This reflected that it was never too late to go down a new path.

My student and I got acquainted while waiting for her instructor to arrive. I learned about the assessment process that would determine the blend of hair dyes that would produce the colour I wanted. My personalized formula would be recorded, so anyone who did my hair in the future would have access to it.

Her instructor arrived just as she asked what hairstyle I wanted. I said, "I want a hairstyle that will make me look taller." When the laughing stopped, we decided on the cut together. It was a team effort, which I knew often got the best results. With my choices made, I comfortably sat, watched, and listened.

I was extremely pleased with the results and scheduled regular appointments at five-week intervals. At the start of every visit, Jeanette welcomed me with her engaging smile, called me by name and remembered I liked my coffee black. It did not matter what the weather was like on my appointment day, I would always leave feeling like the sun was shining.

Of course, the students' self-confidence, attitude, and people-skills varied. The journey they were on, would teach them much about themselves and life. I felt that as a client, I needed to work on staying open to newness, being patient, and precisely convey what I wanted. It made me extremely happy to support them in their growth and development.

A most memorable student was Julie from Quebec. She was wise beyond her young years. She offered me a scalp massage. This was new, an added touch that the other students hadn't provided. I wanted to give it a try. When she was done washing my hair and began the scalp massage, it felt heavenly. I asked if she had training. She said that the technique came naturally to her and that she enjoyed her client's reactions.

Many students and supervisors shared their personal stories with me. Some made me laugh out loud, while the sadness of others made me hope they would find ways to heal their brokenness. There were times when I would pass along some threads of wisdom that had been imparted to me. I shared that, you're not a failure if you don't finish something you started when it no longer feels right. I voiced it was sad when people lost their way because they were trying to meet someone else's expectations.

On going, I would meet another new student and be with them until they graduated. I never tired of repeatedly giving wishes of congratulations.

I wished I had more cash flow when it came to tipping. To show my appreciation, I would give an affordable amount of cash and add to it what I deemed to be my cookie currency. Amazingly, peanuts were never an issue. I was always prepared to ask about another favourite sweet in case they were.

I increased the number of my cookies that I brought when I found out they were being shared among the other students and staff. Their thankyous were heartwarming to hear. I learned that long exhausting days could hamper getting something to eat. One student claimed, rather dramatically, that my cookies had saved her life. Of course, this caused laughter from many. Hearing that my cookies had brightened their day always brightened mine.

The time came when I relocated to a different area. I felt sad to no longer be a part of this world that brought me much pleasure. I was grateful to take with me fond memories. It was the instructors and Jeanette that I would miss most, they were a constant source of delight in my life. I got emotional when they sincerely told me that I would be missed and added so would my cookies.

Taking care of my hair, brought compliments. Whenever asked, "Is that your hair colour?" I would answer wholeheartedly, "Yes, it is." and would follow up with, "I paid for it, therefore, it's mine." This sparked laughter and perhaps was thought-provoking.

*****

I once experienced an in-home shopping party pertaining to the importance of committing to follow a regime of facial skin care. A representative of an established line of skin products was present and took the attendees through the steps of daytime and nighttime treatments. I gave it a try. Then fate intervened, and the absolute perfect product line found me.

To be closer to her new home, my daughter found a nearby location to provide massage therapy treatments. This center was well known for hair and aesthetic services and was pleased to also have Amanda's expertise available to their clientele. There, she met Jennifer Gordon, the aesthetician. They were both passionate about promoting well-being in others. Their friendship blossomed into a business partnership. Amanda gave a lot of thought to the name of their shop. 'Breathe' quickly became a must for many, with its skillful RMT and exceptionally talented aesthetician. Amanda and Jenn had created a utopia of caring, pampering, and rejuvenation.

Their growing clientele derived immense pleasure from the treatments offered. I became one of them and actually got addicted to Jenn's amazing pedicures.

It was Jenn who introduced me to an incredible skin product regimen. To show my appreciation of the care and kindness she gave to me, I gifted her many peanut butter chocolate chip cookies. I also made cookies for her family. Her children's eyes would grow big when I came through their door with them.

On one of my many visits with Jenn, I told her that I was going to donate my cookies for fundraising purposes. I asked what she thought would be a fair price. She replied instantly, saying, *"one million dollars."* I gave her a thank-you hug and then asked her to consider my question more seriously.

Jenn opened the cookie container I had brought, selected one, and mimicked the motions of a wine tester. Then she said, "Okay, I'm being serious, absolutely one million dollars." We both had a great laugh. I never did get an answer I could use, but I did know that we both felt rich every time we were together.

I feel that whether you want to age naturally or give Mother Nature a little help with turning back the clock, surrounding yourself with people who make you feel good, breathes fresh air into your spirit.

Life is filled with losses and wins. Of course, I can't win the war against aging, but I can celebrate my victories on the battlefield of aging.

Chapter 16:
Choices, Gratitude and Closure

My only dream in life had been to love and to be loved by a husband and the precious children we would have together. Life taught me that it can take years to understand and accept that some dreams are meant to be altered.

At sixty-one, I took time to ponder my past before making a crucial choice. It would test my ability to cope and to continue moving forward with my life.

I had met a guy briefly at a summer job and our paths crossed again when I became a full-time employee. Having never been asked out on dates, I was charmed by his interest in me and his gifts of valentine and birthday flowers. He told me I was a good listener. Without any romantic setting, one day he said, "I love you. Will you marry me?" I said yes.

I thought my dream had come true and trustingly handed over my life and weekly paycheques to my husband. He managed all of our finances. I waited excitedly for the day to come when I would quit my day job to be a full-time mom.

During those years, I saw Skip doing his best to make a good impression in his interactions with others. However, it seemed to exhaust him. I thought that being a dad would energize and spice up his life. It took seven long years, then miraculously we were blessed to become parents. I joked that I had been promoted to my new job as a Secretary &

Family Affairs Facilitator. I would be on call twenty-four seven.

The pitter patter of little feet brought sunshine into our kitchen. Our table became that of one in a boardroom, where important construction of puzzles, and Lego blocks could be viewed and celebrated. Also completed art projects and photos would be proudly displayed on our refrigerator. I thrived on meeting the needs of my husband and children.

My husband and I listened to our children's ongoing hopes and dreams, giving our approval, and support. As our children grew, so did their keen spirit of adventure and discovery.

I believed that a loving family could overcome any and all difficulties in life. It was heartwarming to see our two little ones reach out to make their dreams come true. Their piggy bank savings empowered them. They would have money to put towards a special toy or something else they wanted.

The man I married had past issues, as did I. However, I was filled with optimism that together we would become stronger. He was intelligent and worked for a solid company that paid well and offered exceptional health care and a retirement plan. A loving home awaited him at the end of each workday. Sadly, more often than not, a tired, agitated husband and father would come through the door.

Our children were shining examples of how much fun it was to live in the present, but their dad was not of that mindset. Then I thought that maybe he had a medical condition of chronic fatigue syndrome or diabetes. After much coaxing, he went to our family doctor and had blood work done. I received a call that it would have to be redone because of a high alcohol content.

When the results came back from this one, existing physical health issues were ruled out. His doctor then suggested that he see a psychiatrist. After approximately a year of visits, this doctor recommended attending an Adult Children of Alcoholics group. He said this could help to minimize stress in order to invite better days. I was grateful these doctors were being so thorough; it gave me hope. My husband went to a few sessions and declared he didn't need it.

One night, in the quietness of our bedroom, I told him I wanted to make possible a family trip to Disney World, Florida. He was a 'maybe some day we will' kind of guy. As expected, he said this adding, "There's no money for that." When I assured him that I had a one-year plan to earn enough money to cover it, he got agitated. He told me he needed to get some sleep and turned his back to me. I lay awake, feeling more determined.

I brought up my plan again in the light of day, telling him that our children would be so excited to go to Disney World. I added that I thought he too would be since he spent many hours drawing, cutting out, and painting wooden Walt Disney characters. Our children heard our conversation and jumped for joy chanting, "We're going to Disney World." Their dad told them it would cost a lot of money; they assured him they had lots saved up in their piggy banks.

I felt that we all deserved a magical getaway. I gave it some time and then asked Skip to go to the travel agent with me. Knowing this was not going away, he agreed, and our trip was booked. I earned money selling my crafty things and temporarily took in a few school age children. Family and friends also got on board and gave Marc and Amanda money for their birthdays.

When it came time for the last piggy bank count, my children boasted that they were rich. Each had in the ballpark of $150.00.

We counted the sleeps to our much-awaited departure. When it arrived, we headed to the airport with grins on our faces and bags packed with summer clothes, sunscreen and bathing suits.

We basked in our fun-filled time in the magical kingdom enjoying rides and parades. We also met Mickey Mouse and other characters, including princes and princesses. Skip seemed to be having fun and this made me and our children happy. We returned home with fantastic memories of our holiday together.

As time passed, unfortunately nothing really had changed with my husband's frame of mind. In fact, his moods grew darker. I was determined to not give up on him. This went on for years. I convinced myself that I had to accept who he was and that it could be worse as the adage goes.

A blue-eyed little schoolboy, Kenny Crooks, had brightened our household at a time most needed. We lived in a split-entry house, just around the corner from his home. One early Monday morning, this little guy arrived, surprised to find that the wrought iron railing at the top of the stairs had been replaced by a wooden one. His eyes were fixed on it as he made the climb. After reaching the top, he looked at me and said, "Nice fence." Moments like this were hilarious. Then came the day when he was self-sufficient, and no longer came.

After Kenny left, my focus shifted back to the dreadful state of my marriage. We did not live in a climate of impending earthquakes, tsunamis, or typhoons, but I felt the tremors of a devastating force that could shatter my life and that of my children.

Aggressive bill collectors began to call with threats of repossession. This horrified me, so I approached my husband hoping to find a solution. I reminded him that in the past our heart-to-heart talks helped us work through difficult times. Frustrated and angry, he let it slip saying, "I would tell you what I thought you wanted to hear to shut you up." This was a crushing blow.

It was then I told him that what had been intended to be our forever home would have to be sold, before the bank took it. His response was, "Then where are we going to live?" I answered honestly that I didn't know, but what I did know, it would not be together. He turned and left the room. That evening he was the one saying we have to talk. It began with, he would give me a chance to change my mind. I was speechless.

We had accumulated a lot of things over the years and trying to think of what to take with me and what to leave behind was overwhelming. Finally, I told myself it was important to take a good attitude to build a better life, and to leave behind that part of me that would have perished trying to help a man who did not want to be helped by anyone.

Once I accepted that our marriage was without the possibility of reconciliation, I was better able to move on.

I held no bitterness or hate and was comfortable to gather as a family to celebrate occasions such as birthdays and Christmas. It would be at his apartment or a nearby restaurant. I was protective of my independence and never invited him into my new home.

*****

When my phone rang, I was not surprised to hear Skip on the other end. I thought it was about an upcoming event. Instead, he gave me the upsetting news that he had been diagnosed with prostate cancer. He had contacted our children to tell them of his cancer and that it was treatable; they were relieved. I knew he had allowed his car to fall into disrepair and was forced to have it removed from his apartment parking lot. It was not surprising to hear him tell me that he hoped I would drive him to his treatments. I agreed to give him a helping hand.

Then shortly after these treatments ended, another possible cancer was suspected by our family doctor. His suspicion was confirmed, and Skip was quickly referred to a throat specialist.

He wanted me to go with him. This was now becoming a heavy weight to carry. I reflected upon my mom's acts of kindness and remembered her saying throughout my life, "What if that were you?" I also considered that my son and daughter loved their father and needed someone to help him. They had always been there for me, and I owed them. I would be their eyes and ears. I called their dad and said I would take him to his appointment and any tests that were needed.

A specialist ordered additional tests before setting into place a treatment plan. With the results back, he asked for me to be present in his office as he delivered the news. It was a darker day than I could have imagined. Yet another cancer was found on the wall behind one of the lungs. He said both cancers were treatable but required different treatments. He made it clear to Skip his weakened state of health was an issue. The doctor then said that he would have to confer with his colleagues.

I saw the first sign of fear on Skip's face. Our children were shocked and worried. My involvement would escalate. It was stressful, especially knowing he had no one else firmly to depend on. My inner strength was being tested to continue to be there for him.

It was encouraging to hear Skip being told that a team of doctors had been assembled and he was their captain. Together, they would get the best results possible. Having spent a significant part of my life with this man, I knew that he was not a team player. These doctors offered valid reasons to make healthier choices at this critical time; he dismissed their recommendations.

A nurse who was aware of my situation, confided that she too had faced a similar circumstance, and felt no regret for not helping her ex-husband. I however, trusted that my decision was the right one. To cope with the stress, I attempted to compartmentalize what was happening with him from the rest of my life. When given instructions by medical staff, I clarified that we were no longer a couple and that I was there to make sure he had resources to draw from.

I watched him as he constantly stood his ground with the doctors and nurses, refusing to get a flu shot and defending his drinking and smoking habits. I focused on the importance of getting him to and from his appointments.

The sincerity and patience of the doctors and nurses did not go unnoticed by me. To thank them, I packaged my cookies air-tight and began to hand them out.

These men and women were superheroes. My cookies were a total surprise. When I said, "These are for you", there was excitement and glowing smiles. Some said they would take them home to family, while others said they would enjoy them at their next coffee break. Their responses lifted my spirits.

However, I was beginning to feel like I was holding on by a thread. The cancer unit was no stranger to me.

Sitting in the waiting room was a dizzying reminder of my mom's cancer struggles. Again, I saw patients slumped over in wheelchairs or leaning into a loved one for support. On this day, after Skip's assessment, he would be admitted for a brief hospital stay to revitalize his body. I waited with him until an attendant arrived with a wheelchair.

Getting out of the parking lot for me had been a nightmare. Not being able to reach the ticket slot from my driver's seat, an older chap manning the booth would slip it into the slot for me. This day he was not present instead, there was a younger guy. I asked for his help. He glared at me and said, "It's not my job." He then turned his head away.

This was very upsetting. My vehicle was too close to open my door, so I had to maneuver over to the passenger side, to leave through that door. I walked sideways to insert my ticket. When I returned, he took my money and closed the window. The bar went up and I thought so did my blood pressure. I pulled away feeling agitated and would report this incident.

I fell into bed that night, exhausted and knowing I would have to return the next day. Rested and in a better mood gave me an idea for handling the guy at the booth. I was constantly around a lot of people suffering, and just maybe this young guy was dealing with some serious issues.

I, too, was guilty of not always being in the best frame of mind, and undoubtedly caused grief and frustration to others. This is that part of being human that a lot of us wrestle with.

The next morning, my hospital visit was brief. Skip was on intravenous and was drifting in and out of sleep. Nearing the booth, I allowed enough space to open my car door, get out and insert my parking ticket. When the young man told me how much I owed, I asked if he liked peanut butter and chocolate. His eyes narrowed as he guardedly said, ''Yes'' Hearing that, I handed him the money along with some of my cookies. He took both, looking perplexed. I drove off feeling much better and hoped he did too.

The following day, after another hospital visit, I stopped at the booth and was about to get out of my car when the young attendant asked me to hand him my ticket. He leaned out and inserted it. While taking my money, he said, "Good cookies." His eye contact and those two words meant a lot to me. His heart had not turned to stone. This would be the last time we would see each other.

*****

When Marc got the news that his dad was back home, they kept in close contact by telephone. He encouraged him to not give up. My son was often frustrated that his dad did not engage fully with life. Sharing his malaise, he once said, "It's like he has no fighting spirit." I knew my son had been carrying this burden for many years.

Determined to impress upon his dad that his life was worth fighting for, Marc set into motion a plan to come to Canada with his wife, Reika, and Reina, their precious little girl. The thought of meeting his granddaughter was the needed boost. However, their arrival was several days after Marc's dad had been readmitted to the hospital.

Marc and his family's travel time exceeded twenty-four hours. Despite extreme exhaustion, they all came directly to the hospital. I thanked Reika for coming. Reina was in my son's, arms as we made our way to his dad's room. He was in a deep sleep, so Marc gently placed Reina beside her granddaddy Skip, where she too fell off to sleep. He awoke groggy and disoriented. Marc said to his dad, "Look who's here." He was astounded to see his granddaughter lying beside him. He mumbled that he must be a dreaming and did not take his eyes off her.

Marc wanted to be close, so he and his family stayed in a hotel within walking distance of the hospital. This allowed for frequent visits throughout the day. Father and son were born on March 12th Their birthdays had been five days prior, so I got a decorated cake, and we sang, Happy Birthday.

An unexpected snowfall created an extraordinary, magical backdrop to their visit. Reina was three and a half and had never experienced snow. She merrily played in it. Then her dad and I helped her to make a snowman. Her giggles brought joy and laughter to those entering and leaving the hospital. Photos were taken for her granddaddy Skip to see. He continued to become more alert and verbalized his happiness to be with his adorable little granddaughter.

Amanda was in Calgary with her husband, two-year-old and five month old sons. Based on her dad needing rest, she decided to make their visit shortly after Marc's. Many photos of those magical days were shared with her. Also, Reina could look back on them when she was older. When the time came for Marc, Reika, and Reina to return to Japan, we were all grateful that during this difficult time, we shared some precious family moments.

Ongoing, Skip was confined to his hospital bed and his doctor advised this could become permanent. Then days later, I surprisingly got a telephone call from Skip. He was miraculously alert and said that he had been discharged from the hospital. He asked me to pick him up in a few days for a doctor's appointment. It was mind-boggling to try to make sense of it all. I said I would immediately go to his apartment.

After a quick knock on his door, I let myself in with the key I had. The smell of cigarette smoke filled the air. I found him on the living room sofa with a walker close by. He looked gaunt, sitting there dressed in baggy jeans and what was now his oversized sweatshirt. He told me it felt good to get a break from the hospital and said a nurse would be visiting the next day. He added that a neighbour of his had brought him home and would be checking on him.

Once I was sure that everything was fine, I told him if he needed anything to just call me. As I left through the kitchen, an open carton of cigarettes lay on the counter. After closing his apartment door, I felt this troubled soul was finding comfort in his familiar way.

I called the hospital to find out why Skip had been released. The doctor said he signed himself out against medical advice. He added he witnessed other patients get a burst of energy and do the same. He assured me that a nurse would be visiting and confirmed the hospital appointment.

Early Monday morning, I received a call from a police officer wanting to have a word with me. I was aware there had recently been a rash of car break-ins in my area, so was not surprised to get this call. I was scheduled to pick Skip up at noon and had some time to give to the officer. He confirmed my apartment number and said he would arrive shortly.

I heard the knock on my door, looked out the peep hole, and there he was. Once inside, the officer said he had some bad news. I immediately thought my car had been broken into. He told me that it concerned a death, and we should sit down. This sent shivers through me. He continued on, saying a dead body had been found in an apartment, and that the superintendent provided my contact information. Before the words were spoken, I knew who it was.

I was in a daze as I asked when it had happened. The officer said he had not been on-site and didn't have all the details. He told me an investigation was in progress to rule out foul play, and the body would be transported to determine the cause of death. He then gave me a number to call at the end of the day to confirm that I was next of kin. He said after that, I could make the necessary arrangements. The sympathetic officer stood up, gave me his card, and said I could call on him if needed.

I was alone to process the fact that the body of the man who had been a part of my life for forty-three years was lying in a morgue. I saw this on television shows and now was trying to deal with its grip of being a harsh reality.

I sat motionless in the quietness of what had become my new home, thinking how terrible it would be to die alone. I could feel Skip wanted it that way. He died as he had lived, more comfortable alone than with others.

Pulling myself together, I made the difficult calls to my son and daughter to tell them what had happened. Marc was in a state of disbelief. He said he wished he could come back home but it was impossible. I hoped Marc could find solace from of his recent visit with his dad.

Amanda took the news hard trying to process what happened. I could hear the deep breath she took and in a weary voice said, "Mom, I'll be on a plane as soon as I can." She arrived in Halifax the next morning. Her husband and children remained in Calgary.

My daughter helped me make the funeral arrangements. Her dad would be cremated, and his ashes would be laid to rest sometime in the future. Together we cleared out his cluttered apartment. It was an arduous task. Seeing the walker and multiple packages of Ensure protein drinks triggered many difficult memories. I saw my daughter's pained expression as she went from room to room collecting all the cigarette packages that had been opened and unopened. She threw them all into the garbage. Many times, we looked at each other and headed for the door to get some fresh air and to regroup.

When at last, I handed over the apartment keys to the building superintendent, we welcomed some restful time together.

A few days later, the funeral service would be taking place. My daughter came up with a great idea. We had chosen the characters we wanted to keep and then we boxed the remaining handcrafted wooden Disney characters that her dad had made. She thought he would want others to have them.

There was a small gathering at his funeral service. We passed along Marc's appreciation to the attendees. Each one who came to pay their respects was pleased to leave with a treasure or two of their choosing.

Amanda and I shared a teary farewell at the airport. I would miss her but was glad that she was returning to the comfort of her husband and children.

My son and daughter eventually found the peace they needed to move on from how their dad had lived and died. Importantly, they knew he loved them and was proud of them. I shared their feelings and am at peace knowing I was able to help their father during his insurmountable health issues.

PART II

... the making of me

Chapter 17:
My Short-Bred Recipe

As far back as I can remember I was told to eat this and that, followed by, 'It's good for you and will make you grow.'

Upon thinking about the positive and delightful reactions of gifting my cookies to many, it occurred to me that I was the product of specific ingredients in the making of me.

The recipe of my life started with a blend of homegrown and local ingredients. As I continued to age, I became aware that the spice of newness and adventure was empowering.

My much-needed leavening agent would be a mixture of individuals and experiences that would significantly contribute to the shape and texture of my very being.

Chapter 18:
My Homegrown Entreé

I was born in 1950 in Nova Scotia, Canada. I was timid and wished on stars. Fairy tales with happy endings made me happy. Also, Nature's bright colours, scented wildflowers, and abundance of lady bugs for good luck, gave me pleasure.

Our house was small, and the household income was meager. My stay-at-home mom was devoted and selfless in the care of her children and the man she married. My father professed that his marriage was a fifty-fifty proposition. To him this meant, if he made a mess, my mom cleaned it up, because he smoked cigarettes, she rolled them and he being an avid beer drinker meant she learned how to brew.

On weekends, my father drank a lot of alcohol, which could result in merriment, but more often brought a lot of conflict and unhappiness. Our house was small. The girls' bedroom was next to my parents'. Their arguments would wake me, and I would curl up into a ball under my blankets.

After the voices fell silent, I could sometimes hear my mom weeping. I would then get up and look for her. My bedroom door opened into a small area that was more like that of a mini-intersection than a hallway. A tiny bathroom was directly across from me. To my left was the kitchen and off it, the boys' room. To my right was the living room. Our family of eight filled this small space. Most often, I would find my mom sitting on the living room sofa in the dark; the only light source was the streetlight that stood outside.

In the beginning, she would say, "Don't cry, everything is okay," and send me back to bed. Then one night, after another fierce outburst, I was so upset that my mom made space for me to sit beside her. She didn't burden me with frustration and hate; instead, she gave me comfort.

My mom took me with her, back to her younger days, and shared stories of happier times. She told me of her many brothers and sisters, and that she was like a mom to the younger ones. As I listened to her fond teenage memories, there were no more tears for either of us. She talked about riding in the open air on a car's rumble seat. I liked the idea of a folding back seat that could be tucked away out of sight. After that story, I got a warm hug and headed off to bed feeling much better.

There would be more times when we would sit together, silently catching our breath. When she was ready, my mom would share another story or two. She knew I loved fairy tales, so one night she started with, "I met a handsome prince once." I, of course, was enthralled.

My mom described this prince as very charming and kind. He made her laugh and feel safe. She went on to say that they felt and saw life through the same eyes and with the same heart. Sadly, her parents told her he was too old and would not allow a relationship to continue. My mom stared off into the distance for a moment then, in a melancholy voice, told me it was time for me to go to bed. I pleaded with her to tell me more, so she let me snuggle back into place and continued.

Her prince was determined and told her that he would ask her parents for their consent to marry her. But, as she expected, it did not go well. My mother explained that she was taught to obey, not to defy, and therefore felt bound to accept her parents' decision. Devastated, her prince moved away. My mom told me she never stopped loving him.

During another nighttime chat, my mom told me about a man who pursued her. He had a happy-go-lucky attitude; however, she was not as interested as he was. She joked that had she been, I might not have my fair hair and freckled face. Instead, my hair could be darker. She teased me adding that probably I would be taller. We both giggled.

In time, I would hear about yet another man who wanted to marry my mom. She said he needed someone to take care of him, and she knew she could do that. With the approval of her parents, she gave her life to him, 'for better or for worse'. That man was my father.

Many years later, when I was married and looking forward to having children of my own, my mom called me on the phone. I could hear the excitement in her voice. She told me that when her bus door opened that day, the driver was her long lost prince. She sounded like a teenager telling me that they were stunned to see each other again.

She was giddy, recounting how his familiar smile still made her heart soar. She then settled in the seat behind him as he drove on and happily took turns reminiscing about their times together. He told her he was on his own and invited her to meet him for tea. It was scheduled for the next day. I was thrilled to hear this. I always felt that my mom deserved to be happier. Now, she had a second chance. I waited patiently to hear from her.

The following day, I heard a worrisome tone in her voice. She said there would be no more get-togethers. I listened broken hearted as she explained she had given it a lot of thought and felt that my father needed her. She ended with, "I made my bed long ago, and I have to lie in it."

I began pleading with her, saying it was her chance to live out her days with her true love. With my emotional outburst coming to an end, there was silence on the other end. I waited. When my mom spoke, her voice was almost a whisper as she said, "I just wanted you to listen, not tell me what I should or should not do." This haunted me for a long time.

My mom had defended my father during some of our nighttime chats. She told me he confided in her that his mom had referred to him as a mistake. She also said he was devastated when his brother, Gordon was killed in World War II. From that time on when I saw my father in a frenzy, I would think about what my mom had told me.

I seemed somehow to have escaped most of the many episodes of my father's wrath. I always felt sad for the others who did not. Some good memories of my father stuck with me. In his younger days he combed his hair back; when combed forward, it went to his nose. One time while I was sitting on his knee, he let me put bread wrapper twists in his hair, just like the ones my mom put in mine to make it curly. After the second one, he suddenly stood up and I tumbled safely down to the floor. He told me that he had work to do. My father then put the wrappers in my hand and was gone. My mom and I would look back on that with laughter.

A great memory for me and my siblings involved a particular performance of our father. Often when tipsy, he would do his 'I drink a bit Mr. Bojangles like dance.' He would draw our close attention to the shuffling of his feet and stop. Then he would tap his temple with his pointer finger saying, "Up here for thinking." Beginning to shuffle his feet again, he would point down and say, "Down there for dancing." The gleam in his vivid blue eyes told me he was feeling absolute joy.

Decades passed and then I had to cope with the unthinkable passing of my mom. She struggled with the onset of cancer for several years. When her doctor gave the approximate 6-month timeline she had left, it devasted our family. We would make the most of each and every day with her.

Prior to this, I can't recall ever seeing my mom cope with a serious illness. I would often hear her say that she had no time to be sick. My mom was constantly busy taking care of family and spoiling her grandchildren. She also gave hours to a part time job that she enjoyed. The cancer began to aggressively make her body weak and frail. She fought as long as she could to make the best of her remaining time. It was heartbreaking to see her bad days begin to outnumber the good ones.

My mom stayed in my home for a bit, needing ongoing care. One night, as we lay in bed together, out of the blue she asked me what I thought waited on the other side. I looked at her with a sense of dread. Then, not with concern but with humour, my mom said she'd let me know. She also told me that I did not have to stay in my marriage. I remember her words clearly, "Ellen, you do not have to do what I did." Then she drifted off to sleep. The following day she told me it was time for her to go home.

Once back in her own house, her body declined rapidly. Mom was constantly surrounded by the love of her family and we each took turns holding her hand. With her hand in mine, I tried to be strong but had to leave the room in order to pull myself together. Shortly following, one of my siblings found me on the outside deck and told me I had to go back in immediately because my mom was asking for me.

Once again, her hand was in mine; she struggled to speak. I bent down to hear her faint voice say, "Don't cry, don't worry." Her final words to me were to be happy. I could only nod, conveying that I heard her. When I found my voice, I promised I would try. Then, painfully, I told her it was okay for her to go. She passed on that day, August 30, 1990. She was sixty-two.

When Mom accepted that she could not beat the cancer, her wish was to be cremated. At that time, the church I grew up in would only perform a funeral service if a body was present in a casket. My mom then decided to agree to the church funeral, saying it would probably make others feel better. At her funeral service, a priest, who was a virtual stranger, spoke of Edith. He described her as a loving devoted wife, mom and grandmother. He added that her beautiful smile would never be forgotten. All this information had been provided to him prior to the service. As he spoke, I sat with my head down.

Then I heard the priest say that Edith had her own life story, and it was not for anyone else to judge or rewrite. My head rose. He reiterated that it was her story. This was a powerful statement. In time, it helped me to not fixate on her difficult life or dwell on the what ifs. Instead, I focused on and got comfort from knowing that my mom had a heart of gold and was at peace.

Following the church service, her body was taken to a crematorium for her initial wish to be carried out.

While our family gathered in our parents' living room, my brother Stan got on the phone to finalize arrangements regarding our mom's ashes. He asked his brothers and sisters if the following Thursday was okay to gather together at her final resting place. We all agreed. As he was about to end the telephone conversation, he realized that date was my birthday. My brother immediately offered to arrange another time. I told him it was okay without putting any thought into it. As our dear mom's ashes were laid to rest in a niche of a cemetery's freestanding columbarium wall, it was then I felt the brutal devastation that forty years before, my mom had given birth to me.

Approximately nine years later my father needed heart bypass surgery, a common procedure at that time. He had boasted and proved over the years that he had the nine lives of a cat.

Never being a churchgoer, it surprised me to hear him praise a chaplain who visited his bedside at the hospital, prior to his surgery. Curious about his potential newfound faith, I asked him if he believed in Heaven and Hell. He looked at me with a grin and replied, "It doesn't really matter because I have friends in both places." I cherish that moment and have shared it with many over the years.

Following his surgery, he was on a respirator. Several attempts were made to get him off it sooner rather than later as my father was constantly trying to free himself from it. His eyes conveyed that he wanted something. Later, we found out what it was. To our surprise, it was not a cold beer or a cigarette, instead his nurse told us he wanted some ice cream.

Throughout my life, I would hear my father say that he did not want a church funeral when he died. Instead, he wanted to be put in a pine box and be in a room filled with family and friends where drinking and laughter were going on. He said that when he began to smell, it would mean the party was over. Throughout the years, he shared his sense of humour and in his own way, imparted seeds of wisdom to me and my siblings.

Our father passed on at age seventy-two while in the hospital. It was in May, the month he was born. His ashes rest next to our mom's. He had requested a plaque be placed there that read, Together Forever.

Life has taught me that good memories are like warm hugs, while the bad ones can be debilitating if held onto.

Chapter 19:
Local Spices of Friends and School

I think my mom kept me home for what would have been my first year of school because I was small. I had four names and throughout my school years would often hear that for a little girl, I had a lot of names. This fueled my thinking that everybody may have been taller than me, but I had more names than them.

My elementary school days unfolded in a very strict traditional Roman Catholic school. The nuns fussed over little me. Lots of hugs meant getting lost in their long black robes with their rosary beads bouncing about.

When Georgie Dunn was four years old, she moved into a house close to mine. We became inseparable playmates and best friends. Santa knew this and once brought us identical dolls and purses at Christmastime. The only differences were that she was a year younger and bigger than me. She and my mom convinced me to have a sleepover at her place. I would learn that there was another difference.

It was then that I would experience the torturous feelings of homesickness. With my pajamas on, I stared out of Georgie's upstairs bedroom window at my mom ironing in our kitchen. A painful lump grew in my throat, and I started to cry. Georgie's kind dad, George, patiently tried to calm me but to no avail. A vivid memory etched in my mind is of him carrying a sobbing me home with his chin resting on my head. My mother's hugs made me feel better. As she tucked me in bed, she said maybe I could try it another time; that never happened.

On another occasion, I had gone a few doors away to play with my cousin Nancy and came running home, excited to have been invited to go swimming at a sandy beach. I got my bathing suit, my towel, the jam and peanut butter sandwich my mom made for me, and off I went. As Nancy's family car was about to pass by my house, I made them stop and let me out.

In junior high, I met Janet Mitchell and Lorraine Ryall; we shared an interest in sport. Mr. White was our favourite gym teacher and coach. He believed in me and said that I had all the mechanics of a good basketball player but needed to be fast and outsmart the much taller competitors. I worked hard and was thrilled to score a point or two.

A year later, Georgie joined us, and we all got to be on the same volleyball team. Georgie had perfected the overhand serve and once brought our team a victory serving nonstop. As for my underhand serve, I had just enough strength to make the ball go over the net, then it would drop like a stone.

High school became difficult for me, sport wise. My height continued to be a huge factor to deal with. During tryouts, few would pass me the ball. I was disappointed not to be chosen for either the A or B basketball teams. However, I did manage to make the B volleyball team. Three things stood out; there was no uniform that fit me, people laughed when I walked under the net, and my position was substitute, often referred to as a bench warmer.

My friends, Georgie, Janet, and Lorraine, always were there to give me their full support, but I knew my school sport days were over. Importantly, what was not over, was our friendship. We continued to hang out together and keep in touch throughout the years.

Chapter 20:
A Flavor-filled
Pinch of Montreal Spice

My friend Janet discovered a seat sale on flights to Montreal and wanted me to go there to a concert with her. Her cousin Jimmy played bass guitar in a rock and roll band. Everything seemed to happen quickly, and before I knew it, I had boarded an airplane for the first time in my life.

I was overwhelmed by the confined space and wanted to get off the plane. While Janet was trying to calm me down, it began to move. When it finally came to a stop, I thought I had another chance to escape, but the roaring engines indicated otherwise, and the plane began to race down the runway.

The steep climb was scary, and the windows provided no view or light in the overcast night sky. It was a relatively short flight but for me it seemed like an eternity. There were times when the plane shook violently. My friend told me not to worry, turbulence was normal and temporary. I remember saying to her that I would never die in a plane crash if I never got on one. Janet seemed oblivious to this as she went on about how much fun we were going to have.

I felt relief when I heard the captain announce that our descent had begun. I would then be back on solid ground. He wished everyone a pleasant stay in Montreal. Janet encouraged me to look out the window which now had something to offer. Any bit of remaining anxiety faded away as I looked down, mesmerized by the brilliant city lights. My whole life up to that point had taken place at ground level and here I was with a whole new view of the world. This was the first time I did not feel like a little person in the big people's world.

We landed safely and received a warm welcome from Janet's aunt and two cousins. After a good night's sleep and a daytime tour, her cousin Jimmy took us into the city to the concert site. He surprised us with VIP treatment. We even got into the band's dressing room.

There I saw band members chatting up their groupie girlfriends, drinking a beer, and getting hyped up for their on-stage performance. When someone announced that it was almost time, the guys stood up and the girls slipped off their laps. These musicians scrambled to change clothes. There I was, staring at them in their underwear. My face flushed revealing my shyness.

We hurried out of the dressing room and got swept into one of two elevators that took us down to the venue. Janet and I were given seats near a huge mixer panel that controlled the stage sound. The place was packed, and when the curtain went up, the crowd roared. I was wowed by Jimmy in his local band. Then the popular band of Mash McCann rocked the stage.

At one point, I turned to Janet and said that there must be an electrical problem because I could smell something, maybe wires, burning. She laughed and said, "Ellen, I think it's weed." This was a memory we would share and laugh about for years to come.

At twenty-one, I experienced that there was a bigger world out there. Janet's cousin would go on to be known as the songwriter and vocalist, Jim Clench. He became bass guitarist for April Wine and Backman Turner Overdrive (BTO).

Many years later, I was on a flight to Calgary enjoying a chat with the guy sitting next to me. He said it had been a sad day for him because one of his favourite musicians had died. When I asked who, I was shocked to hear him say, "Jim Clench, from Montreal." I told him that I had the pleasure of meeting him when he was twenty years old. It was his turn to be stunned. We shared a moment of silence and then our memories of this great musician. I contacted Janet, offering my heartfelt sympathy. She said her family was devastated from this huge loss.

Chapter 21:
Stirred by Zesty
Scotland Karate Spices

In the first four months of my karate training, seeds of stability had been planted. Then a golden opportunity knocked on my door to test my ability to better handle my life and emotions. Our dojo, along with others, were invited to partake in a Chito-Ryu Karate Do Clinic being hosted the following year in Fife, Scotland. I was astonished to hear this. I grew up knowing that the name of my province, Nova Scotia, meant New Scotland, and had been told that my family name of Brewer went far back to Scottish ancestors.

Randall MacLean, a brown belt who also skillfully managed the affairs of the AKC, would be coordinating and taking care of the travel arrangements for those attending.

Sensei Delaney along with Sensei Gascoigne prompted Marc and me to make the most of this once in a lifetime experience. Occasionally I fantasized about going, then felt the grip of unease to travel so far away. Also, the reality was that, at the time, I had limited access to money in my home. Marc was very keen to go so I would focus on helping him and the others who would benefit from the karate training and adventure that awaited. I planned three fund-raising events.

On many occasions whether at karate class or on the way home, my son would say, "So, are you coming with me?" The most I could give him was a maybe. Then, feeling more confident, the next time he asked, I said, "Yes" He was ecstatic. My mindset then focused on what needed to be done. I took comfort in knowing that I would be surrounded by some of my dojo classmates. This trip necessitated getting a passport which was something else foreign to me. Randall pointed me in the right direction. It was an interesting process which included a photo being taken prohibiting a smile. Conveniently my son at age fifteen would be on my passport. With all of this taken care of, it came time for the flights to be booked. It was then I discovered all the others who had committed early on to go had genuine reasons to withdraw. I was wrecked. Sensei Delaney told me to look on the bright side, saying the available fundraising dollars would further reduce the cost of the plane tickets for my son and me.

Today, I shake my head looking back at how nervous I was before leaving for the airport. I can't count the number of trips I made to the bathroom. A neighbour had come to wish my son and me a safe trip. After waiting for a bit, she had to share her message for me from the other side of the bathroom door. Marg told me not to worry and to have a great time. She ended with, she looked forward to hearing all my stories.

I began to pull myself together on the drive to the airport. Once there, my twelve-year-old Amanda handed me a card she had made and told me to read it on the plane. I slipped it into my purse and gave her a big hug. Everyone at the airport was brimming with excitement and ready to head to the plane that would take us to Scotland. After our goodbyes, I watched my daughter and husband fade out of sight. Marc and I then followed the others.

Our flight was approximately six hours nonstop to Glasgow. With boarding complete, everyone seemed to relax. The guy with the window seat in our row, introduced himself. Russell Hovey was friendly and likeable. I was in the middle and Marc sat comfortably in the aisle seat. I took out Amanda's card and read, "Mom, don't worry about me. I want you and Marc to have the best time and take lots of photos. Love, Amanda xo's." I was already missing my sweet girl.

Shortly after takeoff, Marc told me that his stomach was feeling upset. Sensei Robert McInnes, in his nearby aisle seat, tuned into Marc's situation. He got my son to put his head down, assuring him he would feel much better soon. I was relieved when my son finally raised his head, reclined his seat, and fell asleep. I chatted a bit with this sensei who lived in New Brunswick. He told me he was not only looking forward to the clinic but also seeing his Scottish family. Then he too, invited sleep.

As for me, I was filled with nervous energy, so I went on to chat with Russell. Before I knew it, we were landing at Glasgow Airport. Russell's yawns and tired looking eyes got people's attention. It was said more than once, "Looks like you need some toothpicks to keep those eyes of yours open." I then realized because of me this poor guy did not get the sleep he needed. Feeling guilty, I apologized.

It was a sunny day when the plane's door opened. We descended the steps, crossed the tarmac and went through a back entrance into Glasgow Airport. Our group easily cleared Customs and a dark haired, mustached Paul Hynd was there to greet us. I enjoyed his charming Scottish accent as he guided us to a white minibus with Dunfermline written on it.

When our luggage was stowed, he got into the driver's seat and proceeded to drive on what I considered to be the wrong side of the road. It was a little unnerving, but soon I was distracted by the vast, rolling, rich green pasturelands and grazing farm animals. At one point, someone called out, look at that. There, before our eyes, was a goat resting on the thatched rooftop of a small hut. Laughter filled the air.

Our destination was the home of Sensei Christina and Sensei Fraser Clark, who was the Chief Instructor of Chito-Ryu Karate in Scotland. I had the pleasure of meeting them briefly in 1992, during one of their visits to Canada. Here they were beaming as they announced that the karate clinic would start the next day.

Everyone was delighted to learn that Sensei Shane Higashi, the Head of the Canadian Chito-Ryu Karate-do Association and Technical Advisor of Karate Canada, would soon arrive from his home in Toronto, Ontario. We gave him a warm welcome, and then went off to get settled into our lodgings. My son and I would be staying at the home of Paul's kind-hearted mum, Janette.

The plan was for us all to gather for an evening meal where we would meet our fellow Scottish karateka. The eating establishment was cozy, but I had no appetite. Sensei Higashi got up from his nearby table and came my way to ask why I wasn't eating. I was having a bout of nervousness and I suspected he sensed it. He suggested I try to eat something and then get rested. The end of meal signalled it was time to head back to our designated homes to sleep and ready ourselves for the following morning karate training.

I started to feel better, getting caught up in Sensei Fraser Clark's impactful method of teaching and demonstrations.

It was then I realized that Sensei Paul Hynd was indeed a very capable black belt.

Paul also proved himself as an amazing tour guide. I got to explore the country I had read about and seen photos of in history books. The look and feel of Scotland was a medieval experience to behold. It was unbelievable to me to be standing in the huge, stone Dunfermline Abbey, built in 1128; the final resting place of Robert the Bruce. We visited the humble home of Andrew Carnegie. I learned that he had left due to health issues and became a famous American industrialist and philanthropist. I was told he never forgot his roots and gave back generously to his country of Scotland.

When our training time permitted, we began to break up into groups with those who had mutual sites in mind to see. Russell, Jocelyne LeBlanc, her brother Julien, my son and me began to spend sightseeing time together. We were all from Nova Scotia but meeting for the first time. We walked the famous Royal Mile leading to the historic Edinburgh castle. Along the way there was a tartan shop where I found out about my family name of Brewer. A young Scotsman in a kilt told me it was a small clan that had joined the larger Drummond Clan. He showed me and my son the tartan which was dominated by red and black plaid. Reaching the castle, built on rugged high ground in 1103, left me feeling gobsmacked, as they say in the UK. It was the first castle I entered in my life.

We had a great time with our Scotland karate family which included a pint or two at their local Old Pub. I enjoyed high tea, the taste of haggis, and leisurely strolls in Pittencrieff Park. There, my son and me were fascinated by the gigantic rhododendron trees. These were definitely not like our bushes back home. We also visited the town of Stirling, and lovely St. Andrews by the Sea. I can never forget the sound and smell of diesel fuelled cars on the cobblestone streets of Scotland.

When the time came for our goodbyes, everyone thanked Senseis Fraser and Christina for hosting a remarkable clinic. Back at Glasgow Airport, we handed over our tickets to Dale Proctor who was also from Nova Scotia to be processed as a group. Unfortunately for me and Marc, there was to be a big glitch.

I handed over our itinerary. A search then ensued for me and my son's tickets. I quickly checked my purse, then got on my knees hoping to find them in my carry-on. My friends gathered around me. Russell, who I had kept sleep-deprived, had become a great friend. He sensed my escalating panic and reassuringly said, "Don't worry, you're not alone." He then looked at his watch and added, "Well, not until boarding time." Russell had shown me his humorous side many times over, and this brought laughter. The reality was our tickets were in my suitcase, which was in the cargo bay of the aircraft.

At the check-in counter, an airline agent told me I was in a serious situation. I expected to be helped not confronted with the costly purchase of two new plane tickets. She said this process could be time consuming and I was at risk of missing the flight home with my friends. It was then that I went into panic mode. She excused herself saying she would return. Every second felt like an hour. I hoped I could survive this horrific dilemma. The agent then returned and without explanation quickly began to issue two replacement tickets. Once done, she said, "You'd better get going. Your plane is waiting." I went from absolute dismay to eternal gratitude.

My son and I ran across the tarmac and up the stairs just before they were removed. Panting and out of breath, I was so relieved to be aboard. We were greeted with cheers as we found our seats. I literally collapsed into mine.

After getting airborne, Dale told me that Sensei Higashi wanted to see me. He was seated at the back of the plane, dressed in a black long-sleeved shirt and black pants; his arms were folded. Looking me in the eye he said, "I heard someone misplaced their flight tickets." I immediately and sheepishly said, "That was me." While I struggled to stay calm, he told me to go back to my seat, rest, and to stay there until he arrived. I was curious but was not about to question him.

Our group would transfer planes in Toronto and then head home to Nova Scotia. My son and me had been the last to board the plane and would be the last to deboard while we waited for Sensei Higashi. He walked with us to Customs. I then understood, he wanted to make sure there were no further unforeseen issues. For this, I was grateful.

After wishing everyone a safe trip home, Sensei Higashi asked me to mail my original flight tickets to him. I would waste no time in doing that. His last words for me in the airport were to stay with my group. Sensei Higashi then left to be picked up by a family member.

Despite my airport tribulation, I returned home with great memories, trinkets, and new friendships. I had successfully battled my fear of flying across the ocean.

Jocelyne was much younger than I, and yet we had so much in common. She confessed that she also had been nervous about committing to the Scotland trip.

Weeks later, I got a call from Jocelyne. Before it ended, she promised to drive from Digby County to Halifax to visit me and Marc. I then contacted Russell who lived near our International Airport to see if he wanted to hang out again. He gladly accepted the invite. We shared more happy times with laughter that often took my breath away. Our friendship is one that endures a lifetime.

Chapter 22:
A Dash of Bittersweet Seasonings

I was on the road to being more self-sufficient. I learned to assess and do what I could responsibly, without having to always depend on others. A local grocery store incident put me in a 'I can do this' frame of mind. The item I needed sat high beyond my reach. With no one near to help, I decided to hold on to a sturdy nearby post and ascend a shelve. As I stretched to reach my favorite tomato sauce, a store associate approached.

He asked sternly, "What do you think you're doing?" To me, it was obvious. He immediately extended his hand to help me down. Once my feet were planted back on the floor, he looked down at me and asked what I wanted. He reached for the bottle of sauce with ease. He handed it to me, along with a loud and clear message, one you might give to a child, that I was to never do that again.

On another occasion, I would be the punchline of a joke in a drug store that I had never visited before. I asked an approaching associate for the location of a product, then noticed the nametag in her hand implied she was either on a break or her day was over. I told her that it was okay, and I would find the item I needed. She was exceedingly kind and insisted on showing me where the hair products were, so off we went.

As we were about to pass by the pharmacy counter, someone behind it called out, "I thought you were off work." The associate teasingly said, "I am, but I decided to help this woman and, as you can see, I am much taller than her." With that, raucous laughter broke out, loud enough to be heard throughout the store. This was their joke, not mine, and obviously my feelings were not taken into account.

These two experiences indicate how I can show up in the world, so I thought of a way to add to this.

For instance, when someone helps me, having a higher reach than mine, I thank them. Then I offer my assistance to them saying, "If you drop something, I will gladly pick it up for you because I'm closer."

A blend of logic, coupled with a good sense of humor can be most enjoyable and rewarding.

Chapter 23:
My Two Favorite Take-Out Deliveries

I have often heard pregnancy humorously referred to as having a 'bun in the oven'. I always wanted to make and give birth to at least four babies. It took a long time before I felt the first flutter of life inside me; it was like that of butterfly wings in flight.

I was disappointed to be given the news from my doctor that due to my slim hips I would never be able to naturally deliver my babies into the world. It was while writing this book that I found some humour in the fact that my son and daughter were 'take-outs' by a surgeon and 'deliveries' to me by a nurse.

I feel blessed to have children that are the sweeteners in the 'recipe of me.'

My son, Marc was hungry to become an inspiring teacher. The completion of a Master's degree and PhD made it possible for him to get a position as an assistant professor in a reputable college in Japan. He is enthusiastically engaged in his career as an educator and facilitator. Marc also, continues to thrive in his karate training and related endeavors.

My daughter Amanda sold her partnership in the shop of Breathe, to enjoy being a devoted full-time mom to her children. She is also a very enthusiastic and caring volunteer in her community of Legacy. Amanda further satisfies her craving to brighten the days of others with her gratifying hobby of creating inspirational customized jewellery and accessories.

Chapter 24:
Medley of Worldwide Travel Invites

Throughout my childhood, there were no family vacations. In my marriage, there were some nearby outings which included my families annual PEI campouts. Therefore, when it came to travel, 'the recipe of me' was flavoured by my children's life choices and my treasured abundance of dear international friends.

I loved welcoming others into my country, my home, and my heart, and never thought beyond that. The invitations extended to me to visit them in their home countries continue to amaze me.

I got to climb the many steps of the Eiffel Tower with Delphine and her Olivier, to enjoy the view of the wondrous city of Paris spread out below. This was followed by an evening boat cruise on the Seine taking in the brilliantly illuminated bridges, the Louvre, Musée D'Orsay, and other famous sites. I marvelled at finding myself standing inside the Opéra de Paris. I rode in a car around the mighty Arc de Triomphe, strolled along the famous Champs-Elysées, and explored the opulence of the palace of Versailles and its vast beautiful grounds. I also sat dreamily in a pew of a most famous cathedral of the Middle Ages, Cathedrale Norte Dame.

One day as our picnic on a riverbank in Mériel came to an end, Delphine asked if I wanted to see the church Vincent Van Gough painted in the last year of his life. My answer was a wishful, yes. It happened to be a short walk away. When I neared this church in Auvers-sur-Oise, I felt the enduring strength of its simple stone structure and as I sat in a pew inside, a peacefulness swept over me. Following, a five-minute walk took my friend and me to the resting place of the famous painter and his brother, Theo.

On another visit, I was delighted to find myself within the walls of Claude Monet's Giverny home. I was impressed with his enchanting gardens and crossed an authentic Japanese bridge that spanned a section of a pond where water lilies flourished. Images of Monet's famous paintings were present everywhere.

Normandy was emotional for me to visit, conjuring up a place where many lives were lost. Etretat then calmed and welcomed me with its beauty. I explored the inside of a cliff's tunnel-like opening that took me to the other side to enjoy another view. Then I climbed the high cliff and gazed down at the brilliant, tall, white stone structures jutting out from the clear water below.

The South of France charmed me with its beaches in Nice and Cannes. I swam in and enjoyed the buoyancy of these salty waters of the Mediterranean Sea. I was elated to be with Fabien and Sylvie again, and to be in their lovely new home in Biot. From there, we traveled to his parents. Marie-José and José's gorgeous villa in nearby Vence, sits on the edge of a deep ravine. I descended a spiral staircase within their home that led to a small room full of a variety of musical instruments; Fabien's family love music. I thanked his sweet mom and his dad for sharing years of their son with me and my family. Their hospitality was endearing. A tour of the principality of Monaco, the Mediterranean city-state famous for its wealth, grandeur, royal family, casinos, and motor sports was a most welcomed surprise.

I would return to the South of France again years later, happy to spend more time with my French family. This also gave an opportunity for my travel friend and me to board a swift train to Italy. Rome, the Vatican, the Sistine Chapel, and innumerable other historical sites were no longer places I had heard of instead, they became places to savour.

I have a vivid memory of a dazzling sight. Into the night, after climbing up steep subway stairs, I was captivated with a spectacular close-up view of the ancient Colosseum. It was illuminated and still wet from a rain shower; the night's air was fresh and intoxicating.

I spent two sunny days in Venice and fell under its spell, while walking over quaint arched bridges, one being the famous Rialto bridge. In its public square, Piazza San Marco, I fed the pigeons that gathered round. Seeing a nearby wedding party celebration, with its gaiety, felt dreamlike. I glided on quiet side canals where no motor craft is permitted. The very charming gondolier skillfully maneuvered his boat while sharing stories of the famous Marco Polo and Casanova. He pointed to where they had stayed.

Added to my travels was a road trip invitation from a friend. These few weeks in the USA, started out with a flight to picturesque Salt Lake City, Utah to pick up a vehicle and drive back to Canada. We travelled through sixteen states.

Our time outs from the road brought about amazing sights and enjoyable interactions.

There were many highlights, like experiencing the energy of Las Vegas in Nevada. Travelling Route 66 felt surreal. I enjoyed Texas with a sleepover in El Paso. Another thrill for me was to walk along Nashville's main street knowing singers continue to seek their musical careers in this place. The vast sunbaked deserts and long winding railways conjured up childhood memories of western movies on a black and white television. The Hoover Dam was impressive on the ground and from the sky above. I also was enthralled with the magnificent sight and depth of the wonderous Grand Canyon while standing at its edge. During this trip, I saw the unique enriching vegetation and animal life of the swamps and marshes of the Louisiana wetlands. The variety of entertainers and visitors in New Orleans were enjoyable. I have a great memory of engaging with a French mime. An overnight in North Carolina gave me a spectacular view of the Great Smoky Mountains.

Throughout this USA adventure, many evocative song lyrics danced in my head. I actually was standing on a corner in Winslow, Arizona and breathed in the sight of, 'almost heaven, West Virginia, Blue Ridge mountains ...' just to name a few.

The music and cultural lifestyle worldwide is certainly amazing witness up close.

Before boarding a cruise ship, I was invited to spend two days in the popular Key West. Its streets were alive with partygoers and music. I also was elated to visit Ernest Hemingway's home. To walk through the rooms of this great author's estate, was a privilege.

During the Caribbean cruise, my travelling companion and I were entertained, well fed, and welcomed into four ports of call; the Bahamas, Mexico, Grand Cayman, and Jamaica.

The balcony off our cabin offered a personal space to relax and savour life's pleasurable opportunities.

Many travel ingredients have enriched the 'recipe of me' and I have an appetite for more.

My friends made it possible for me to not only grow, but to travel throughout the world, not as a tourist but as a fellow traveller. The gratitude I feel is beyond words.

Chapter 25:
A Sweet and Sour Blend
Food for Thought

"The best laid plans of mice and men often go awry" was adapted from a line in "To a Mouse" by Robert Burns. Its meaning became a harsh reality for me.

My plan would start with a week in Taipei with Mei's family, and then two flights to my son's home in Kumamoto, Japan. It was time for a family reunion. I looked forward to seeing Reina and meeting my grandson, Kenshi, for the first time. He was almost two. The well-planned gatherings of my international students and their parents for us to spend time together were set into place. Three glorious weeks would also include a visit with Soke and others I had met in 2002. I recall thinking how wonderful life can be.

A few days before my flights to Hong Kong and Kumamoto, my plans changed drastically. I experienced the most terrifying episode of my life. Word spread rapidly of the 6.5 and 7.3 earthquakes that took place on April 14th and 15th in my son's city. The images on the news broadcasts were chilling. Sitting on the sofa in Mei's home, I watched and listened, unable to process the horror of it all.

Lives had been lost. The evacuations continued and Kumamoto airport was shutdown. Age-old sacred buildings had fallen, and land travel was risky because some roads no longer existed. Along with this, I learned a series of aftershocks would be felt.

Thinking of my son and the what if's was crushing me. I needed to hear his voice, but his cellphone was unresponsive. When Marc finally was able to contact me, he sounded very distraught. Like many others, he and his family evacuated their homes to sleep in their vehicles, not trusting the safety of their houses. I sighed a breath of relief knowing they were safe while my heart ached for all those dealing with this nightmare. My son promised to keep in touch as much as possible. Amanda and I kept in close contact, comforting each other.

Mei's family was supportive and exceedingly caring. I was welcome to stay in Taiwan. Throughout my life, I had been told that I think too much so I was grateful for the distractions Mei's family kindly provided to keep me from doing just that. I had come laden with gifts, including canned lobster, so I busied myself preparing a box to mail to Marc, Reika, Reina and Kenshi.

On that day I needed some alone time and didn't join Mei and her mom on their outing. As I bent down to get something from my suitcase, I experienced a sudden and frightening up and down motion. I staggered to my feet. Then everything started to sway back and forth; the windchimes jingled eerily. Instinctively, I ran from the room and almost collided with Mei's brother. Yin-Min had been coming out of his bedroom directly across from mine. He was calm and spoke his first English word since I had arrived, "Earthquake"

I followed close behind him, then sat on the sofa as he continued on to the kitchen. He returned with some water and headed back to his room, totally at ease. I had heard Johnny Cash's song, 'The Ring of Fire' but, I would apply a new meaning to those words. The Ring of Fire is another name for the Circum-Pacific Belt, which is the epicenter for ninety percent of the world's earthquakes. Earthquakes in that vicinity are an accepted way of life for many.

Mei and I returned home to Canada on our originally scheduled flight. I sat on my sofa, depleted. Life had delivered my son, his family, sister, and me a cruelty we could never have imagined. I was still struggling with bouts of anxiety.

As I thought of those grieving tremendous loss, especially of their loved ones, while cleaning up and rebuilding, I felt a great admiration for their fortitude. Their actions inspire to step up, not to give in dire situations.

Chapter 26:
My First Taste of a Karate Takedown

Friday nights were open for extra karate training and many belt levels attended. My son used this time to prepare for tournaments; he competed in kata and kumite events. I was fascinated with kata but nervous about kumite. I used this extra time to improve upon my techniques. Sensei Higashi had once expressed that much practice is needed when learning but it must be perfect practice. This resonated with me.

Kata is a series of perfectly executed techniques used in the face of danger against an imaginary assailant. Kicks, punches, blocks, among other perfect techniques, are executed. As I watched various katas being performed, I could visualize the battle going on.

For me, sparring meant the physical act of fighting. Because I did not consider myself a fighter on any level, I knew it would be one of my biggest challenges. In class and at tournaments, I saw kumite in action. I marvelled at the delivery of lightning speed techniques. In competition and karate workouts, there is never an intention to cause bodily injury. The quality of the technique is never compromised therefore, a safe distance is determined for controlled light contact. I had observed that in competition, the application of weak or poor technique was not acceptable, and neither was a bad attitude. Warnings and penalties are given accordingly. This was good to know but did not encourage me to participate.

One Friday night I had the opportunity to practice Rendori. A familiar black belt said this exercise would help me considerably. It consists of two people using attack and defense techniques. It starts with one initiating an attack while the other blocks and counters with their attack. This continues for a count of fifteen. Before the exercise begins, the participants mutually agree to a nonstop rhythm of movement. I requested a slow pace.

We found a vacant space in the middle of the dojo and began with a ceremonial bow to one another. My awkwardness indicated I had a lot to work on. When we were finished, Sensei Paul Tyson bowed and assured me that, with determination and practice, I would become more comfortable and skilled. I remained fixed in the spot we had occupied, observing my fellow karateka who were committed and focused.

Then my eyes came to rest upon a physically fit, thirtyish-looking guy in blue jeans and a t-shirt. He bowed as he entered the dojo in sock feet. There was something familiar about him. He stood along the walled perimeter observing. Much to my surprise, he removed his socks and then walked towards me. I recognized that he was Sensei Golz who I had seen at clinics. He asked me if I wanted to spar.

I stood frozen as my mind began racing. I thought it would be disrespectful to decline his request, then I heard my voice timidly say, "Sensei, I am not very comfortable when it comes to fighting."

He looked at me reassuringly and then got into position. I mirrored his arms by his side, palms touching his *gi* pants, heels together and his feet at a 45-degree angle. Then we bowed to one another to begin. I concentrated on my footwork, moving forward, backward, and side to side; always maintaining a safe distance. Then he quickly moved in on me and, just like a scene in the Karate Kid movie, down I went. He extended his hand and helped me to my feet. I was sure he easily read the 'I was not expecting that' look on my face. He said, "You have to be ready for anything."

As our sparring continued, I wished I could some day be more capable of perfect timing and skilful techniques. I went on to be evasive. Then, down I went again. This time I got up quickly on my own and became much more engaged. After a few more exchanges, Sensei Golz indicated the exercise was over. I believe he knew I had learned a valuable lesson. He wished me a good evening, then left me with his impactful words, "You're not as powerless as you think you are."

I began to concentrate on the value of *Shin*, 'Spirit, Heart, and Mind' along with the mindset to be more physically and mentally ready to engage in sparring. As time went on, as the saying goes, I got more experience under my belt.

During one of my regularly scheduled karate classes, we were continuously rotating to work with a variety of partners. After a ceremonial bow, I looked up at the tall, adult black belt standing before me. I would be sparring with Sensei Dean Kenley who was from an outlying dojo. I moved about the floor, assessing and looking for an opening to attack. He was lean and aggressive, delivering excellent techniques. I would feel their touch, proving that he was a master of perfect distance.

Sensei Kenley was very flexible. He easily and flawlessly delivered mawashi geris (roundhouse kicks). As he started yet another, I saw my opportunity and knew I had to be fast. I watched his right leg rise with his knee bent, centered to his body. As he pivoted on his left foot and was extending his right leg for the kick, I moved in quickly. With his leg resting on my left shoulder, he was then supported by only his left leg. My timing and distance gave me an open target to deliver a punch to his abdomen. This was proof positive to me that I was making progress, and that my short stature at times could be used to my advantage.

*****

Randomly my cousin Allison and I met again; this time it was at a karate gathering. It was there I learned that Allison's boyfriend, Chris had started his karate training in the AKC at age thirteen; he got his black belt and went on to start his own dojo in East Hants. Allison told me they had met through Sensei Delaney and his wife, Cheryl. She then pointed to Sensei Golz saying, he was now her husband. This felt like a moment in a fairy tale.

My son and I had seen him at karate clinics, never knowing we had something special in common.

Fun visits to the home of Allison and Chris ensued along with outstanding karate workouts at his dojo. I excitedly welcomed them into my home.

Believing in myself is an important ingredient in the 'recipe of me'. It warms my heart that Allison's Chris was the one who told me at an open Friday night karate session that I was not powerless.

Chapter 27:
Powerful Leavening Agents
Help Me Rise and Shine

One night, after my karate class in Sensei German's dojo, he asked me to consider competing in the Women's Masters Kata Division at the Soke Cup Chito-Ryu Karate Do 10th International Championship. This competition had started in Japan in 1983 and would take place at three-year intervals. Then, it was decided to give outside countries an opportunity to host. In 1989, the competition took place in Vancouver, Canada. Three years later it was back in Japan, then in 1992, it was hosted by Australia then back to Japan. This cycle continues with a variety of countries offering to host. The date of the upcoming one would be in Kumamoto, Japan, August 2010.

Immediately after my next class, Mitchell took me for a coffee to follow up on the seed he had planted. I told him it was far beyond what I thought I could do. He then gave me valid reasons why I should reconsider, starting with he believed that I could do well in the competition. He ended with, "Do you think someday you will regret your decision to not compete?" I was consumed by everything he had said.

When Soke arrived in Nova Scotia for his annual karate visit, as always, I had a supply of my cookies to give him. We enjoyed our frequent chats, and on this particular visit he would hear something totally unexpected from me. I told him that I was considering competing at Soke Cup. He beamed and said, "You are tiger, you strong." If I stepped up, this would be my first time ever to compete in a karate competition. Over the years Soke and I had learned that we both were born in 1950. He emphasized that 2010 was in a Year of the Tiger. Following our conversation, it then felt right for me to compete. I began extra training to reinforce my decision and help reduce the nervousness within me. Ultimately, I would focus on bringing my best to the competition floor. I chose Seisan kata, which I had admired watching others perform from the very start of my exposure to karate.

Our Canada's Karate Team East travelled together and stayed at the same hotel in Kumamoto. We practised in the hallways and at the Sohonbu dojo that I had visited 8 years before. Being an athlete instead of a volunteer, made for an entirely different feel and I liked it.

We met up with Canada's West karate team from British Columbia. The Olympic Winter Games had been hosted there earlier in the year. They brought 'Believe' hats and t-shirts of that time to share with their fellow Canadian athletes, and I was one of them. Marching in, representing my country filled me with a sense of pride I had never known. We wore our red team jackets along with our crisp white competition gis.

When it was my turn to compete, I entered the ring wearing my brown belt and with a determined voice, announced my chosen kata, "Seisan" I demonstrated attacking and defending techniques as best I could. Upon completion, I awaited my score. I left the ring feeling on a high, having achieved what I set out to do.

I would again see those amazing people I had spent time with in Scotland seventeen years prior. Senseis Fraser and Christina Clark were dignitaries at this Soke Cup. Sensei Paul Hynd, like my son and me, was a competitor. With the competition over, it was time to relax and to celebrate being together at Soke Cup.

That evening we reminisced about our time in Scotland. My Scottish friends then admitted they were shocked to see me compete. I will never forget their sincere praise.

Christina took me aside saying, "Ellen, I don't think you realize what you have achieved, and it may take a long time for you to totally understand the significance of it." Her words proved true. For sure this felt surreal at the time and then became another defining moment in my life.

It had never crossed my mind that, weeks before celebrating my 60th birthday, I would be standing on a podium in Japan receiving a bronze medal. A little girl, who could have lived, struggled, and died in her own limited little world, got to see and feel the world in a bigger way.

I consider my medal as one of courage, and I am filled with pride knowing that I eliminated a regret that no doubt, would have haunted me.

Soke and Sensei German encouraged me to rise to a huge challenge. I am forever grateful to have these amazing men in my life.

Chapter 28:
Nova Scotia Karate Team Wholesome Blends

1994 was an exciting time for my son and me. He worked hard to become a member of the Nova Scotia Karate Team and I worked diligently behind the scenes, fundraising and giving help to all those who needed it. Coach David Griffin, a well known and admired Sensei, asked me to assist him and the athletes at the upcoming annual karate competition.

The Canadian National Black Belt Karate Championship was taking place at the University of Calgary. It would be my first time to be in western Canada. I flew on my own and would stay in the downtown hotel with the team. I was grateful to be present for my son's first competition at this level. I also felt fortunate to wear a Nova Scotia team tracksuit.

It was a monumental experience for me to be in the marshalling area where chants rang out from every provincial team. Then, little me was handed our big Nova Scotia flag to lead the march in. I was giddy that such an honour had been conferred on me. The flag's size was challenging, but when I was cued to start walking and heard the 'Eye of the Tiger' song blasting throughout the venue, it energized me to hold our flag high.

I proudly led our athletes in and around the perimeter of the large competition floor and planted our provincial flag among the others. Ever since then, hearing the Eye of the Tiger song transports me back to that amazing time.

I cheered on our Nova Scotia athletes and took pride in their victories. It was indeed a thrill to see my son presented with a team event bronze medal. After this eventful competition, I wished my son, the competitors, and coaches a safe journey home.

My friends, Jocelyne and Russell, residing in Prince George, British Columbia at that time, travelled to take in the event. Following it, we grabbed a few days to explore. We were wowed by Banff and Lake Louise with their magnificent mountainous backdrop and savoured the natural beauty of the Rockies. Upon our return to the hotel, we unexpectedly met Sensei Higashi in the now quiet lobby. He invited us to go up the Calgary Tower to see the stunning panoramic view, and then to enjoy a meal together at a favourite spot of his. Time had passed quickly since our shared Scotland days. We embraced yet another opportunity to spend together.

I was asked to be the manager of the Nova Scotia Karate Team in 1995. It felt great to officially be part of this dynamic team. I would give my best to meet all responsibilities, adding media attention to the list. I considered my position a privilege not a job. I would be among all those with tremendous heart, spirit, and dedication, as they delivered their best in the world of competition. I also got to travel to many hosting provinces within my country and made enduring friendships along the way.

Fifteen years unfolded as I revelled in every moment spent with countless athletes, their supportive families, phenomenal coaches, competition officials, volunteers, and friends. When it was time for me to relinquish my duties as manager, I was pleased to hear that Greg DaRos, a skilled black belt team competitor would take over. I always liked his positive morale boosting spirit.

*****

An amazing memory I would take with me started on a chilly October day in 2000 when I picked up my mail and headed to my car. Like me, it needed warming up, so I took some time to leaf through the envelopes. I was surprised to see one was from Sport Nova Scotia.

It was a letter that started with, "On behalf of the Board of Directors of Sport Nova Scotia, I would like to congratulate you on being selected as Volunteer of the Year by the Nova Scotia Karate Association. Your accomplishments over the past twelve months have been most impressive and the award is well-deserving." The second paragraph went on to say, "You will be honoured at the Investors Group Awards Luncheon." The last paragraph finished with, "Congratulations on being counted among Nova Scotia's finest."

I remember being absolutely stunned and having to read the letter a second time. This recognition left me speechless. I noticed Cherry Whitaker, Chief Instructor of New Glasgow Karate Club and current President of the N.S.

Karate Association had been cc'd. I admired how extremely capable she was in all of her endeavors pertaining to karate.

In mid-November, Cherry and I would be joined by my son, Marc and my daughter, Amanda as we sat at one of the many round tables. This large room was crowded with athletes, coaches and guests. I did not feel deserving to be there until the recipient of Athlete of the Year gave his heartfelt speech. In his moment of glory, he thanked Sport Nova Scotia and his coaches. Then this young man said that without his parents' selfless support, the availability and maintenance of the ice rink, lights being turned on, the doors unlocked along with other essentials that he would not be standing there. He was in the limelight yet took time to express his deep appreciation to those behind the scenes.

The end of his speech was followed by a brief silence and then everyone stood up and began to applaud. I believe they, like me, were feeling humanity at its best. Reaching great heights most often comes with the collective effort of many people behind the scenes.

Chapter 29:
Karate Tidbits
I Recommend You Sample

The two amazing young men I met when I began karate are in my opinion, the salt of the earth. I saw their friendship feed off one another as they went on to achieve much success in their lives. This includes having their own karate dojo. They wholeheartedly teach Chito-Ryu Karate Do to those coming through their doors. Once roommates, they now live many provinces away from each other.

Canada East In 2005, Chief Instructor Sensei Mitchell German established his own Chito-Ryu Karate Do dojo. I felt privileged to lend a helping hand with its start-up and the design of the club crest, proudly worn on the gis of his students. Sensei German is an outstanding person. He has several experienced instructors in his Halifax Ryuseikan Karate Club, located in Cole Harbour, Nova Scotia. His membership continues to grow, and the successful, life-changing feats of his students are known locally and worldwide.

Canada West In 2006, Chief Instructor Sensei Gary Sabean established his own Chito-Ryu Karate Do dojo in Calgary NW. A few years earlier he had relocated to Alberta and then decided to make it his home. This was to support his wife's chosen profession and happily he became a stay-at-home dad to their two daughters. He is dedicated to his students and their training at The Sabean Karate Academy. The membership continues to grow which is a testimony to his character and expertise as a skillful teacher.

Mantra

I wrote this Japanese haiku early in 2020 to help me cope with the shocking presence of the brutal Coronavirus Disease (COVID-19)

Talk Less Listen Learn

Take Responsibility

Act Do not React

Epilogue

My book culminated into a testimonial to many and a legacy of my life. Among these stories are others that I hold dear. I feel grateful to have been motivated and shaped in a positive way. Kindness and gratitude opened many doors for me to walk through, to connect with others, and to flourish.

Our daily lives can be demanding, and periods of time can roll into years. I decided to reconnect with those I had lost contact with, and together take a stroll down memory lane.

It started with an old-fashion telephone call to Ontario, Canada. It was heartwarming to hear the voice of a man who had a significant impact on my life going back approximately thirty years. Sensei Higashi and I shared fond karate memories and then we updated each other with family and current events. As our conversation was coming to an end, he said, "Ellen you have climbed to the top of the mountain." Hearing this from him made my heart soar.

I used Messenger to contact Sensei Paul Hynd. He did the math and concluded that it had been twenty-seven years since our first meeting at the karate clinic in Scotland. Our karate kinship held treasured memories to re-visit and enjoy. Several times he said fondly, "It feels like only yesterday." When I told him I was writing this book, he said he would pass along this exciting news to Sensei's' Fraser and Christina Clark. The next day he delivered their sincere heartfelt wishes. I continued to reach out to others who had been important in the 'making of me'. All our exchanges were joyful. Some told me that they were going to do the same and get in touch with others whom they had in mind.

Writing this book at my age has been most challenging and, with its completion, another growth spurt for me.

The ingredients of my parents and siblings, my marriage, my children, and grandchildren blended together with good friends went into the 'making of me'. The icing on top includes my study of karate, confidence building, international friendships, and world travels. My ongoing recipe of Ellen Brewer Waterfield continues to improve and welcomes more ingredients into the mix.

I am grateful to have learned that my past and shortcomings did not have to define or limit me, unless I let them. People come in different shapes and sizes, with weaknesses and strengths.

The aging process has decreased my stature to four feet, seven point eight inches. Fortunately, being little is no longer a concern of mine. I have come to understand that in life, you do not have to *be* big to *think* big.

I believe wholeheartedly that you should never underestimate yourself and that it is never too late to own your journey.

My Peanut Butter Chocolate Chip Cookie Recipe

Ingredients:

2 Eggs

2 ½ Cups of white flour

1 Cup of softened butter

½ Tsp of salt

1 Cup of light brown sugar

1 Cup of white sugar

¼ Tsp of baking powder

1 Cup of smooth peanut butter

¼ Tsp of baking soda

2 Tsps of vanilla

Semi-sweet chocolate chips

Pre-heat oven to 350 degrees Fahrenheit.

Method: In a mixing bowl thoroughly combine softened butter with peanut butter. Add sugar, eggs and vanilla and blend ingredients for a smooth texture. Combine flour, salt, baking powder and baking soda then add to mixture.

With cookie batter in hand, roll into small balls; arrange on a cookie sheet evenly spaced apart. Then lightly press down with a moistened fork. Place your desired number of chocolate chips on top.

Bake for approximately 11 minutes (suggest rotating after 9 minutes for best results) Let cool for a bit then place on a baking rack.

Makes approximately 4 ½ dozen cookies depending upon the size of rolled batter. These cookies are freezer friendly.

Tastymonial

Westphal Dental   •••
Jun. 5, 2019 at 8:59 a.m. · 🌐

We are so lucky to have wonderful patients! These are
THE best peanut butter chocolate chip cookies in the
world! Thank you Ellen Waterfield🍪

Enjoying Nanny-Ellen's cookies in Kumamoto, Japan.

"100 thumbs up!" in Calgary, Canada.

Japan, 2002

Soke Cup, Japan 2010

Santa wearing his black belt and me with my green.

My Dad's favourite flowers.

Acknowledgements

Thank you, Marc, my dynamic son, and Amanda, my amazing daughter for your ongoing love and support enjoying good times and getting through the bad times.

Thank you, my party of five dynamic grandchildren. Domo arigato gozaimasu to my daughter-in-law, Reika for Reina and Kenshi (Kumamoto, Japan) Thank you to my son-in-law, Mark for Devon, Logan, and Clara (Calgary, Canada) We are family!

Thank you to my Nova Scotia family for happy times shared, Gordie & Linda, Stan & Lynn, Celie & Gerald, Holly & Robert, Eldred & Anita, and all my nieces and nephews

Domo arigato gozaimasu to Soke, Master of the International Chito-Kai (son of founder, Dr. Tsuyoshi Chitose of Chito-Ryu Karate Do) and family members for your hospitality during my 2002 visit. Also, Domo arigato gozaimasu to Takatsuau, Nakayama Sensei, Hidemichi Kugizaki Sensei, Hiroshi Tanaka Sensei, Masataka Matsuzaki Sensei, and Kawazu Michiyo for your kindness. Domo arigato gozaimasu Seiichiro Nanai Sensei and Sensei Sandra Philips (Australia) for your encouragement

Thank you to all of my fellow karateka in Japan, Hong Kong, Australia, Norway, Scotland, Ireland, the USA and Canada

Thank you, Dr. Robert Scovil, Dr. Rob Miller, Dr. David Whitby, Dr. San Fung, Dr. Stephan Roth, Augusta, Lawyers Lisa Teryl, and Shawn Scott and Marie & Dale Lowe for your professional and personal support

Thank you, Sue Goyette, David Weale, Allissa Blondin, Robin Albright, Joanne McKenzie, Gordon Michael, David Walsh, Rob Cutler, Robert Molaison, Brian & Norma Cannon, Irene Cawdell, Joy Sutherland, Marg Weatherbe, Richard Landzaat, Bill Hildreth, Ivan Burt, Al Gallant, Malcolm MacDonald, Julie Rosseau, Ivan Osadchuck, Bob Shelton, Jeanette & Vennie Gray, Steve & Christie Crawford and Millie Campbell Mercier

My sincere appreciation and thanks to Heather Andrews a dynamic human being and Publisher, and to her team for helping me to share my stories on the pages of this book.

About the Author

When Ellen arrived for a short-term stay in Calgary Alberta, there was no guarantee of what awaited. However, she believed everything would work out as it was meant to be. It began with being situated a short walk away from her daughter. Along with its single bed, Ellen added a desk and computer. Framing her new space was a big window that would let in the sunshine and blow in fresh air for daily inspiration. She started to write this, her first book, in that quiet little room.

Ellen quickly experienced the warmth of the diverse population in the Community of Legacy SE Calgary and participated in ongoing gatherings of celebration. Alexandra Velosa, a devoted organizer, befriended her.

Ellen felt fortunate to be in a socially active community. However, neither she nor anyone else could have imagined the onset of a worldwide health crisis. Humanity would have to dig deep to cope with fear and grave uncertainty.

With strict safeguards set in place and promised vaccines, people in Legacy capitalized on using the technology at hand to reach out and support one another. It included uplifting messages and generous neighbours leaving needed groceries for another on their doorstep. Birthday street parades were organized with multiple vehicles driving by with horns honking and people waving. This was to reassure that the special day did not go unnoticed. Ellen discovered a Ninja had left a note and bag of goodies with her name on it at the front door of where she was living. Creative ways to show caring abounded.

Ellen made life changing decisions which included coping with living far away from her family and friends in Nova Scotia

She is happy to be a resident in the Community of Legacy. As a Calgarian, her cookies are now brightening up the days of others and opening more doors of conversation and connection.

Manufactured by Amazon.ca
Bolton, ON